RETRO CHIC

**A Guide to Fabulous Vintage
and Designer Resale Shopping
in North America & Online**

BY DIANA EDEN & GLORIA LINTERMANS

Printed in Toronto, Ontario

10 9 8 7 6 5 4 3 2 1

First Printing: October 2002

Library of Congress Cataloging-in-Publication Data
Retro Chic: A Guide to Fabulous Vintage and Designer Resale Shopping in
North America and Online
By Diana Eden and Gloria Lintermans
285 p., 5 x 7 in.
ISBN 1-893329-15-1

Cover, design, and illustrations by Ingrid Olson, Tülbox Creative Group

Visit our web site at www.ReallyGreatBooks.com

To order Retro Chic or for information on using copies as corporate gifts,
e-mail us at Sales@ReallyGreatBooks.com or write to:

Really Great Books
P.O. Box 861302
Los Angeles, CA 90086

RETRO CHIC

A Guide To
Fabulous Vintage
and Designer
Resale Shopping
in North America
& Online

TABLE OF CONTENTS

This book by no means represents all of the fabulous stores available across North America and on the Internet. The authors have selected their favorite stores or stores for which information was readily available. Every shop has something unique to offer, and the fact that not every one of those listed is personally reviewed is only a reflection of space limitations on the page and the impossibility of personally visiting each. The authors hope you will like their selections and forgive the omissions.

Any indication of "current" offerings is merely to help define the type of merchandise offered and can only be indicative of what was available at the time of writing, and therefore may not be available upon publication of this book.

Unless otherwise stated, all stores take major credit cards.

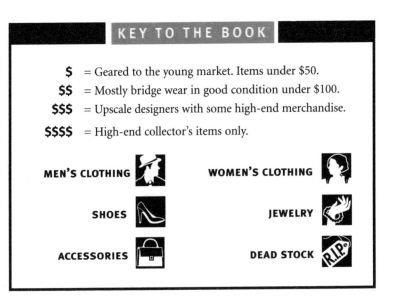

KEY TO THE BOOK

$ = Geared to the young market. Items under $50.
$$ = Mostly bridge wear in good condition under $100.
$$$ = Upscale designers with some high-end merchandise.
$$$$ = High-end collector's items only.

MEN'S CLOTHING

WOMEN'S CLOTHING

SHOES

JEWELRY

ACCESSORIES

DEAD STOCK

ACKNOWLEDGEMENTS

Diana Eden

The envelope please. My thanks go to my brother Bill and sister Carol, for providing me with a home while I researched the Canadian stores, to my researchers Monique Lyons and Natalya Brown, and to my loyal Sandy Lane, who keeps me sane and organized. Thanks also to our agent Charlotte for her unique character, encouragement, and guidance, and to Mari, who loved our project from early on. Special thanks to my husband Dominic, who provides me a safe place to do the creative work I love to do, even if it's seventy hours a week. To Gloria, who generously shared her plan for this book with me, and has always inspired me to trust her completely, not something I do easily, I offer my heartfelt and incredibly deep gratitude.

Gloria Lintermans

To my first best friend, my dear sister, Marsha, whose support during overwhelming times has been and continues to be greater than I can express, and to Gail and Linda for being there, even when I was buried knee deep in research to the point of distraction, thank you. My thanks to Charlotte, my fabulous agent, for her dogged determination and belief in this project, Mari at Really Great Books for her tremendous insight and ongoing support, Susan the world's best editor for her keen eye and tireless attention to detail, and Tabitha in Seattle. To Nina for her enthusiasm, to Richard, Evan, Amy, and Jeana—Jeana, your knowledge of the vintage and resale scene in New York City was invaluable and I can't thank you enough for your dedication to the cause…and my entire family for their support. And to a very special woman, Diana, my co-author and friend, for your knowledge and wisdom. You have been a joy to work with from start to finish, and I thank you. Most of all, I dedicate this book to my late husband, Rick, for all your patience, love and unwavering support.

The authors would like to thank:

Harmony Downs, Kristin Petersen, and Madalena Romero for support. Interns Lindsay Blumenfeld and Anjali Kumaran for their commitment to accuracy. Publicist Brian Gross and sales associate Janelle Herrick for aiding the project's success on so many levels. Ingrid Olson for her production and artistic talents. Anna Kevorkian for her meticulous eye. Mari Florence for making it all possible. And editor Susan Jonaitis for her ongoing dedication to this book and our sanity.

O ver the last decade, the demand for vintage and resale clothing has exploded. Today the most dazzling stars and supermodels can't get enough of it. Winona Ryder almost single handedly launched the retro craze by wearing vintage outfits to high profile events, and other celebrities followed eagerly. Sharon Stone, Cameron Diaz, Nicole Kidman, Melanie Griffith, and Julia Roberts all create their own unique style using vintage clothing.

Fabulous looks come from understanding the difference between fashion and style. When Edith Head, the renowned costume designer for the film *Roman Holiday* first saw Audrey Hepburn, she immediately prescribed what were then called falsies (to amplify the size of her breasts) and caps for her teeth. Hepburn stood her ground, not only rejecting faux curves and caps, but also insisting that not a single hair be plucked from her generous eyebrows. Head regrouped and reassessed. She recognized that Hepburn "was a girl ahead of fashion, who deliberately looked different from other women."

Hepburn credited designer Givenchy for "creating" her look over four decades, but her image was her own doing. She stripped away distracting accessories, chose to wear her sweaters backwards and rejected cumbersome stiletto heels for ballet slippers and flats. She knew what worked for her: what beguiled and what enhanced.

Today, with all of the eclectic fashions of the 20th century to chose from, no period is off-limits—and every decade can be found in a variety of wonderful vintage stores in this book.

The late Pauline Trigère, the French-born design pioneer who helped define American style between World War II and the tearing of down of the Berlin wall, has reached fashion icon status all over again in the designer resale market, as trendsetters like Naomi Campbell hoard her vintage dresses, tops, and capes.

The '60s fashion designer, Mary Quant, has her own take on why fashions from this decade, for example, are so popular again. "I think because the '60s were so optimistic. The '60s were a revolution in so many things…theater, art, film, photography. A youth quake—the '60s burst through, particularly with fashion. It was fashion to live in and dance in."

The '70s are clearly still with us in wrap dresses, popularized then and now by Diane von Furstenberg, the highly collectible status of Pucci prints, and the prevalence of flat-front, low-rise pants.

Classic pieces from the great designers of the 1980s are still very much in demand—Galliano, Lagerfeld, Yves Saint Laurent, Versace, Valentino, and the still superb Giorgio Armani. These pieces are timeless, wearable, and popular—as the owners of these stores will tell you, they cannot keep Chanel, Fendi, or Gucci bags from the '80s in stock.

Part of the costume designer's art is mixing old and new pieces to create modern looks, not just characters for period films. These designers, from Gilbert Adrian and Irene to today's crop of talent, are intensely aware of the connection between fashion and film, drama and design.

Although you might expect to see period garb in Woody Allen's *The Curse of the Jade Scorpion* set in 1941, would you have thought Oscar-winning actress Helen Hunt would be wearing a vintage dress for scenes in the contemporary film *As Good As It Gets?* Or that many of Dharma's outfits, in the TV sitcom *Dharma & Greg*, are vintage pieces mixed with items bought at local department stores?

Join us as we explore the must-shop spots we have fallen head-over-heels for in Los Angeles, New York, San Francisco, Seattle, Dallas, Chicago, New Orleans, Boston, Toronto, Montréal, and many more. In each city we guide you to both vintage stores (for treasures from designers and decades past) and designer resale markets (for contemporary high-end designer clothing at a fraction of the retail cost).

For shoppers who love to hunt from the comfort of home, we have included an extensive chapter on shopping the Internet. Color photographs of vintage and couture clothing and jewelry are just a mouse-click away.

In addition, check out the Vintage Expos, where fashionphiles from around the world converge to find genuine treasure. And don't forget the auction houses such as Christie's and Sotheby's and eBay® online which are now introducing very popular vintage and collectible fashions.

Ready? Grab your measuring tape and join us as we sail through fabulous stores in major U.S. and Canadian cities and a veritable cornucopia of on-line treasuresthrough cyberspace.

ENJOY THE HUNT!

—Diana Eden & Gloria Lintermans
Los Angeles, 2002

DESIGNS AND DESIGNERS OF YESTERDAY

THE '20S

The years between the end of the Great War and the beginning of the Great Depression are famous for the styles and fads of the Lost Generation. Flappers, gin parties, the Charleston, jazz, the rise of gangsters, and the arrival of "talkies" all mark this era.

In 1920, women gained the right to vote with the ratification of the 19th Amendment. Nothing in the 20th century would have such an impact on women or the clothes they wore. Ready for emancipation, women's clothing abandoned the genteel fashions of the pre-war years with its corseting and other painful manipulations of the female figure. Freed from their corseted curves, a silhouette that flattened the bust and ignored the waist emerged. Caps and cloche hats, short skirts with fancy gartered stockings, and hip-hugging dresses were everywhere, often trimmed with fur or fringe, and sometimes detailed with Egyptian or Chinese stylings.

Inovations in the transportation industry (primarily the car) caused clothing and accessories to become more streamlined to fit the active lifestyle these modes of transport provided. Women's hair was cut short in bobs, and frequently covered with hats that sat so low no hair was seen, sometimes even their eyebrows were hidden.

In the early '20s the hem was still at the ankle, but it rose and fell as the decade progressed. It hovered at its shortest, just below the knee, in 1926 and 1927. Legs appeared for the first time as a visible part of a woman's appearance, and knees were rouged for an erogenous effect. A slim figure, best set off the look, and there was new emphasis on sports, such as tennis, and the beach, where tanning was for the first time in vogue. Women went to men's shops to buy themselves golfing cardigans and V-neck sweaters.

At home, satin pajamas became popular. Later, pleats, fringe, handkerchief points, and asymmetrical hems were added to the straight silhouette.

Poverty and unemployment plagued much of the population, yet the image of the 1920s as one big party is quite pervasive, and clothing certainly reflected more of the party than the struggle. The passion for dancing, whether the sedate tea dances or the Charleston, necessitated clothing that enabled movement. Evening dresses were short but richly decorated with beads, sequins, or rhinestones embroidered in elaborate geometric patterns. Though these dresses can still be found, they are often very fragile and cannot be worn. However, they are works of art in themselves as decorative pieces and well worth finding.

One of the most influential designers was Coco Chanel, who decided early on that she would "rid women of their frills." She realized that working women sought comfort and simplicity, which she personified in the sweater set, tweed skirt, leather belt, basic black dress, pearls, and short evening dress. Her look was understated elegance, not displayed opulence. Clothing with the Chanel label is still some of the most sought after in vintage and designer resale stores alike.

The Italian designer Fortuny created gowns made from accordion pleated silk that resembled classic Greek costumes. Actress Jill Clayburgh found one in an antique store and wore it to the Oscars in 1976, the year she was nominated for *An Unmarried Woman*, a forerunner of today's trend to dress in vintage for Hollywood's biggest nights.

Men's suiting was typically broad shouldered and loose fitting. Trousers were pleated and reached their widest (about 24 inches) at the same time as women's skirts were the shortest. White was fashionable in men's summer wear—white slacks, white sweaters, even white jackets. Knickers were popular for golf, raccoon coats were the rage with college students, and the late '20s saw the adoption of two-toned spectator shoes for men.

Boué Soeurs: Feminine *robes de style* (a full-skirted, calf-length dress with a close-fitting bodice and natural or low waistline) of taffeta and silk organdy with ribbon and lace trim.

Callot Soeurs: Velvet and lace dresses with elaborate beadwork.

Gabrielle "Coco" Chanel: Wide-legged "yachting pants" and wide-cut beach pajamas—both an adaptation of menswear styles for women's fashions. Belted raincoats, open-neck shirts, and blazers in beige, gray, and navy. Chanel introduced her signature jersey suit; tweed skirt with sweater; faux pearl necklace; purse with gilt chain strap; and the timeless "little black dress."

Lilly Daché: A New York City milliner known for her cloches and turbans with several different colors of velvet twisted together.

Erté: Russian-born fashion illustrator and designer of fantastic sets and costumes for the Folies Bergères revues in Paris. Created stunning evening dresses for Mrs. William Randolf Hearst.

Ferragamo: In 1923 he became a prominent shoe stylist in Hollywood, designing and making shoes by hand for Dolores del Rio, Pola Negri, and Gloria Swanson. Unable to make a profit from handmade shoes because of high U.S. wages, he returned to his native Italy in 1927 and continued to make all shoes by hand. Intent on comfort as well as design, Ferragamo took up to 13 measurements of toes alone.

Hellstern & Sons: Designed shoes, chic boots, and pumps with two- to three-inch Louis XIV heels. Boots for day and evening were a company specialty, including fetish boots with up to eleven-inch heels.

Jantzen: Oregon-based manufacturer, developed the elastic or "rib" stitch used to manufacture innovative swimwear. Introduced an elastic one-piece tunic-style suit that allowed for more body movement. Decorated with three wide horizontal stripes, these sleeveless unisex suits attached to the swimming trunks at the waist. Despite the controversy caused by this new design at public beaches, they sold widely, and their signature patch, a red-suited girl in mid-dive, was seen affixed to cars and other personal belongings, as well as on swimwear.

Jeanne Lanvin: Exquisite embroidery on evening gowns to jackets to negligees. *Robes de style* of 18th- and 19th-century inspiration, including wedding gowns; evening gowns with metallic embroidery; tea gowns; dinner pajamas; dolman wraps; and capes. Also known for the Lanvin Breton suit: a short jacket decorated with small buttons and a large white collar, usually shown and worn with a sailor-style hat.

Jean Patou: Each season he launched a new color: patou-blue, patou-green, etc. In 1924, on a trip to the U.S., he was the first designer to show his collection on American models. Simplicity, sometimes verging on severe, was a keynote of his designs, including tennis outfits worn by tennis star Suzanne Lengler. Other designs included Cubism-inspired sweaters and princess line dresses that gave the illusion of high hips by raising the waistline. Long, simple gowns accentuated his customers' jewels.

Elsa Schiaparelli: First designs were black hand-knit sweaters with a white bow in the design, giving a tromp l'oeil effect. Was one of the first designers to adopt the zip fastener.

Madeleine Vionnet: First designer in modern history to work on the bias. The bias cut stimulated a new recognition of the beauty that a lengthening line can give to a woman's figure. Noted for classical drapery, wide necklines, easy over the head styles, faggotted seams, and art deco embroideries.

THE '30S

America had suffered the Wall Street crash and unemployment was escalating. When big band sound and big screen glamour provided distraction from economic depression, life on film was all top hats and feather boas. Hollywood pulled off the ultimate seduction: style in motion. Visual perfection met eternal beauty on screen. There was no better medium for fashion. Paris had directed for centuries, now Hollywood was poised for world domination.

Women adopted wide-legged pants and the mannish cardigan sweaters that Chanel borrowed straight from the wardrobe of British gentlemen. Lana Turner popularized knits and twin-set sweaters. Cary Grant in a double-breasted suit and Katharine Hepburn in trousers exemplified sophistication and style. After the soft and sloping shoulder drape of the early '30s, the wider, shoulder-padded designs of the mid-30s, popularized by Joan Crawford and Greta Garbo, came to signify the self-assured woman.

The rich might have looked to Paris for their fashions, but couturiers kept their eye on the effect of Hollywood's tantalizing glamour. Clothes relaxed, but with an elegance. Backs plunged on dresses. In Paris, Madeleine Vionnet continued her freed-up silhouette of the bias cut and cowl collar.

The nylon stocking made fashion news along with the introduction of silk and rayon dresses, whose stylings were as varied as their printed fabrics. There were straight skirts with fitted tops, full skirts and blousy bodices, small collars and V-necks, and extra detailing from shoulder pads and fishtails to peplums. The most typical hemline of this decade fell below mid-calf, about 12 inches off the floor.

The use of the zipper became widespread for the first time because it was less expensive than the closures that were previously used. Another innovation of this decade was varying hem lengths for different times of the day—mid-calf for daywear, long for the evening.

Foundation garments took into account the natural contours of the female figure in a whole new way. The outstanding item in loungewear was the pajama, for daytime and evening, formally and informally, in private and in public. Made of soft fabrics, the voluminous trouser legs gave the impression of a skirt as they draped in full folds around the ankles. Swimwear shrunk, now practical enough to finally be used for swimming and sunbathing. Reminiscent of Carmen Miranda films, bare midriff tops made their first appearance.

Important accessories were the belt and hat. Fashion designer Mainbocher, once editor of French *Vogue,* introduced the trademarked "glamour belt," which gave women the ability to instantly change the look of a dress. Belts had detachable buckles and came in art deco geometric designs. There were also small, knitted hats, including berets of Lastex yarns and Schiaparelli knit madcaps and tams. For evening, women wore turbans and headdresses.

Purse styles were varied and often made of colorful suede. Most common were back-strap pouches or envelope bags in cloth and skins. Straw handbags emblazoned with fruits and vegetables were popular along with top-handled purses, zippered pochettes, and crescent-shaped bags. Evening purses were smaller, sometimes made of brocade or needlepoint, some decorated with sequins and jewels. Gloves, essential in any woman's wardrobe, were longer, often with gauntlets, and made in a variety of colors and textures.

As for men's clothing, the double-breasted dinner jacket and Windsor necktie knot practically define the '30s. The bow tie was popular along with a narrow-shaped Indian madras bow for casualwear. Hollywood-inspired neckwear included Humphrey Bogart's narrow, black tie. By the late '30s, polka dot ties were trendy. Trousers featured waist pleats and rode high, and the collarless cardigan sweater, colorful handkerchiefs, argyle socks, and camel's hair coats were typical.

MANUFACTURERS AND DESIGNERS TO LOOK FOR

Gilbert Adrian: Tailored suits with exaggerated wide shoulders, dolman sleeves, tapered waist, pinstripes, or set-in patches of color; dramatic animal prints on sinuous black crêpe evening gowns; mixed gingham cottons; asymmetric lines; and huge ruffle-topped sleeves. Designed the "Letty Lynton" dress for Joan Crawford to wear in the movie of the same name—within just a few days of the movie's release, the New York City Macy's sold a half million copies of it. Adrian also designed for leading ladies Ann Miller, Marion Davies, Katherine Hepburn, and Kathryn Grayson.

Cristóbal Balenciaga: Unusual uses of jewelry, somber colors (browns and blacks), and restrained lines. By the end of the '30s, his suits had dropped shoulders, narrow waists, and rounded hips.

Tom Brigance: Extensive sportswear collection of brightly colored linen separates: shorts, pants, skirts, and bare-stomach tops. Used oversized patterns, geometrics, and large florals, and started the trend for mixing patterned fabrics such as checks and stripes.

Hattie Carnegie: Tailored suits and dresses with straight skirts and the versatile black dress.

Catalina: One of the first makers of mass-produced swimwear.

Gabrielle "Coco" Chanel: Trademark Chanel suit—braid trimmed, collarless jacket, patch pockets; knee-length skirts in soft Scottish tweeds; the introduction of "costume jewelry" such as multiple gold chain necklaces with faux jewels; chain-handled quilted handbag; beige and black sling-back pumps; and, for the hair, flat black hair bows and gardenias.

Jo Copeland: Elegant fabrics such as thin wool woven with gold sequins. Dynamic drapery.

Lilly Daché: Draped turbans; brimmed hats that molded to the head; half hats; war worker's visor caps; colored snoods; and hats made of a mass of faux flowers.

Ferragamo: Handcrafted shoes, originated the wedge heel, platform sole, and Lucite heel. Combined exotic wedges and platforms with the rich costume fabrics of medieval Florence.

Hermès: Accessories with coordinating sports clothes such as purses with watches set in them. Mid-'30s introduced "Kelly" bag—a saddlebag-like design.

Charles James: Heavy silks, ribbons, and fine cloths for elaborate, bouffant ball gowns in innovative mixtures of colors and fabrics; bat wing oval cape coats; intricately cut dolman wraps; asymmetrical shapes; and culottes.

Jantzen: Revealing, clingier swimwear like the innovative "Ladies Uplifter," a body-sculpting suit that enhanced the bustline with darts and elastic and had an adjustable skirt to hide figure flaws. "Wisp-O-Weight" tunic-style swimwear in flesh tones, causing the wearer to appear naked. Incorporated Lastex (U.S. Rubber Co. trade name for elastic yarn fabrics), a new rubber-based fabric.

Louise Boulanger: Superchic elegant dress designs; hems shorter in the front than in the back; gowns cut on the bias with exaggerated, massed fullness at back of skirt and over hips; rich, beautiful fabrics such as flower designs on wrap-printed taffeta moiré for evening.

Elsa Schiaparelli: Used surrealist fabrics designed by Salvador Dali and Jean Cocteau. Thick evening sweaters with shoulder pads; dyed fur coats; Tyrolean peasant-inspired fashions; culotte dress; decorative plastic zippers; lamb chop and ice cream cone hat; handbags that lit up or played tunes when opened; and glowing phosphorescent brooches. Her lasting innovation is the combination of a dress with a matching jacket. One of her famed customers was the Duchess of Windsor.

Valentina: Simple, classic architectural lines. Trademark all-black evening look with gown, cape, hose, and a Maltese cross pendant.

Madeleine Vionnet: Continued to use the bias cut for the total garment as opposed to its previously limited use in collars, sleeves, gores, and borders. Engineered the freed-up silhouette of the bias cut and cowl.

THE '40S

Before the outbreak of the war, fashion was elitist and escapist, ping-ponging from the Paris salons to the silver screen to determine who could outdo whom. Clothes were now part of the rallying cry for unity. Fashion had metamorphosed into a morale booster and government tool. After decades of free reign and decadence, the fashion industry had to be creative within the new constraints of economic responsibility and social rules.

While Britain was buckling down to austerity and clothing coupons, America provided the glamour. *Vogue* reported American woman wearing a "revolutionary new silhouette with sloping shoulders...shirtwaist dresses," which were dressed up with jeweled buttons and whimsical hats.

On June l, 1941, the rationing of cloth and footwear was introduced. Clothing requirements were reduced to 66 coupons, the same quota as magarine. The new attitude was "it looks wrong to look wealthy," and this dictated the new silhouette. Such things as the depth of the hem and belt, the number of buttons, the elimination of ruffles, turnover cuffs, and other unnecessary decorative accents were all mandated by law, especially in Europe. The American government waited until 1943 to impose price controls and restrictions on use of fabric and superfluous trimmings. The style of military uniforms, with their mannish shoulder pads and utilitarianism had a profound influence. Women went to work in factories, for the Red Cross, and driving buses, so their clothes reflected their emerging importance in the workplace. Needed for parachutes, nylon was no longer available for stockings, and in 1943, *Vogue* magazine included a photograph of a model wearing ankle socks!

Because fabric had to be preserved at all costs, accessories became key, yet economics dictated even further compromise like hats that stayed on without elastic. With straw in short supply, the summer alternative became the crocheted snood, wood-soled shoes to save leather, larger shoulder bags to let women become more self-sufficient, and, since dye was in short supply, dull and practical colors.

Cashmere sweaters from this decade were not only luscious to touch but also warm to wear because they were "triple ply," unlike the single or double ply sweaters of today. Women's jackets were either full in the back with a gathered yoke and full sleeves, or very fitted with padded shoulders (padding also added definition to blouses, shirtwaists, negligees, evening gowns, housedresses, and tailored coats and suits). The square-shouldered silhouette, the tailored suit, the military uniforms seen so often during the war. and a mannish stride were promoted by such reigning film favorites as Katharine Hepburn, Marlene Dietrich, Carole Lombard, and Lauren Bacall.

With little time for self-indulgent luxuries, women's hair grew long. Veronica Lake was the model for an exotic hairstyle, parted on one side with a long swooping lock combed forward to hide one eye. This craze caused so many mechanical accidents for women in the new war-created work force that the U.S. government asked Hollywood and Miss Lake to cut her silken locks and change her now infamous hairdo.

Favorite pinup girls were Betty Grable, Hedy Lamarr, and Rita Hayworth. Also popular was a frank and brightly made-up mouth, little or no blush, and eye makeup for dress occasions. Fingernails were painted in brilliant colors.

Leather was now restricted to military use, so shoe designers were forced to be increasingly clever. Every imaginable material was incorporated into shoes, but reptile skins and mesh were the most successful substitutes. Because stockings were also unavailable, women painted black seams on their legs with makeup. Since this wasn't especially practical as an ongoing ritual, ankle socks became increasingly popular.

"Zoot suits" (born around 1935 in Harlem nightclubs) made a brief appearance but were a waste of too much precious fabric. Introduced by teenage male "hepcats" and "jitterbugs," zoot suits had an exaggerated drape-shaped jacket with broad shoulders and extreme length, almost to the knees, and was worn with a huge bow tie and an ankle-length key chain attached to a belt loop.

After the war in menswear, shoulders were broadened and padded, waists were nipped in to a semi-fitted line, and lapels were wide and double-breasted. Trousers were generous in width and pleated at the waistband. A white dinner jacket with shawl collar or a midnight blue double-breasted suit would be typical for evening, as would a Glen plaid or pinstripe double-breasted suit for daywear.

The Hawaiian shirt, picked up by servicemen as souvenirs, became popular casualwear by the late '40s. Post-war fashions contrasted the frugality and somberness of wartime clothing and included brimmed hats, wide collars, walking shorts, and accessories—large cufflinks, plaid socks, and colorful ties.

These ties were wide, at least two to three inches, and are still available in many vintage shops at good prices.

By the end of the war, buoyed by expectations of prosperity and an influx of European talent, Christian Dior's "New Look" (christened by Carmel Snow, editor-in-chief of *Harper's Bazaar*) ushered in the elegance of French couture. With a full, curvy silhouette that was nipped in the waist and full skirts with petticoats, women were happy to return to a more feminine figure. Hemlines dropped from the war time length of just below the knee to the lower calf. Teen culture emerged with rolled-up jeans and bobby socks. The Eisenhower jacket made fashion news. Hollywood played out paradigms of masculine elegance from the rugged Bogart trench coat to Cary Grant's refined black tie.

MANUFACTURERS AND DESIGNERS TO LOOK FOR

Gilbert Adrian: Broad-shouldered suits with long jackets and narrow waist, opulent ball gowns, and draped dresses for evening. Geometric designs for fabrics and patterns of his own design with animal trompe l'oeil or Greek themes. Hollywood's influence on fashion continued with him as he created many memorable clothes for the likes of Ingrid Bergman and Greta Garbo.

Arrow: Popularized the colored shirt for men. Also manufactured ties with zany '40s patterns.

Cristóbal Balenciaga: Jackets flared below the waist; big sleeves; and pill-box hats.

Tom Brigance: Wrap tops that bared the stomach, trousers, shorts, and swimwear. Synthetic jersey fabrics with cotton piqué and prints.

Jo Copeland: Narrow waist-length jackets; asymmetrically decorated skirts; casual and formal evening dresses and suits.

Lilly Daché: Designed dresses to go with her hats, gloves, hosiery, lingerie, and loungewear. In 1949 she designed a wired strapless bra.

Christian Dior: Revolutionary "New Look"—ultra-feminine silhouette using yards of material in an ankle length skirt with a tiny waist, snug bodice, rounded sloping shoulders, and padded hips.

Jacques Fath: Hourglass shapes; swathed hips; plunging necklines; full pleated skirts; wide cape collars; and perfume, scarves, millinery, and stockings with Chantilly lace tops.

Madame Alix Grés: Molded silhouette over an uncorseted body; statuesque Greek-draped evening gowns in cobweb; Alix Jersey (named for her); two-color pleated jersey gowns with criss-crossed string belts; cowled, black jersey day dresses; asymmetric drapes; bias cut caftans; loose top coats with hoods and bat wing sleeves; and beachwear.

Irene: Chief designer for Metro Goldwyn Mayer; slim, softly tailored suits; meticulously cut and tailored slack suits; crisp and functional sportswear; feminine dresses; glamorous, flattering evening clothes.

Norman Norell: Chemise dresses and tunic blouses over slim skirts with belted waist; colored swing coats of various lengths; fur trench coats, pavé sequined sheath dresses for evening; and wool dresses with décolleté necklines.

Pauline Trigère: Simple but dramatic evening dresses in wool and taffeta in a range of styles from long to ballet-length. Used the cut of the fabric to shape garments instead of tucking and shirring. Introduced removable scarves and collars on dresses and coats, and dresses with jewelry attached.

THE '50s

Designs reflected energy, optimism, and kitsch. Youth split their ranks between Elvis-coiffed rebels and the Ivy League. The cinema created heroes out of brooding bad boys. James Dean in *Rebel Without a Cause* and Marlon Brando in *The Wild One* inspired the cult of jeans and motorcycle jackets.

The white T-shirt, once an undergarment, assumed a new mythic level, reflecting the wearer's machismo, rebel status, and low class origins. Glamour itself was redefined in the contrived yet naïve sensuality of the figure-revealing sheath dresses worn by Marilyn Monroe and Brigitte Bardot, whose figures were far fuller than today's fitness standards would suggest.

Claire McCardell's "American Look" of practical separates, flat shoes, and wrap-around dresses in plain fabrics reached a critical mass, and sold across the country through the Fuller Brush catalog.

By the end of this decade, a young Yves Saint Laurent, heir to the late Christian Dior, gave the first suggestion that even couture would take its cue from the street, with a youthful collection of knits and leather jackets. The little black dress was reborn along with headbands, pedal pushers, capri pants, Bermudas, clam diggers, and plaid fabric.

In the beginning of the decade, the silhouette of women's clothing was the hourglass shape of Dior's New Look. Waist cinchers and crinolines were still very much a part of a woman's wardrobe. But the pinched waistline began to disappear as semi-fitted suits with short, boxy jackets arrived in store windows. Looser shapes in bloused-back styles and dresses with dolman sleeves were popular. Cocoon-shaped jackets and coats appeared and waistlines fell to the hips or rose to the Empire line.

By the late '50s, the straight chemise, or sack, arrived with the free-swinging trapeze, or tent dress, and the puffed-out bubble, or harem skirt. The new corsetry controlled and redistributed weight. Dieting became fashionable and *Vogue* featured a 'Skimmed Milk Diet,' 'Measures for the Unwanted Pounds,' and a series on 'Calorie Counting.' Readers were told to "fit the foundation to the fashion" featuring the new rounded bustline and nip-waisted girdle for an emphasized waist.

Leather, Levi's, and Converse sneakers helped create the look of the day. Along with the famous poodle skirts and ponytails, saddle shoes, penny loafers, and colored sneakers were popular with teenaged bobbysoxers.

Men's fashion shifted from a square, broad look to a slender Ivy League silhouette. The well-dressed man might be seen in a hand-tailored suit of Italian raw nubby silk. Evening clothes took on color, and dinner jackets were available in wine, gold, Bermuda blue, silver gray, and Moroccan beige.

MANUFACTURERS AND DESIGNERS TO LOOK FOR

Adolfo: Panama planter's hat, banded in striped ribbon or jersey; the shaggy Cossack hat; huge fur berets; clothing made from packable jersey fabrics; snoods. Imaginative separates, custom-created blouses, and long skirts for at-home entertaining; Pierrot-inspired ruffs at neck and wrist; and soft caftans.

Cristóbal Balenciaga: Free-form demi-fit; the sailor's middy, which became the overblouse; cocoon coat; balloon skirt; short-front long-back flamenco evening gown; bathrobe wrap coat; and the pillbox hat.

Pierre Balmain: Brought French style to American sizes—tailored suits, evening gowns, and sheath dresses with jackets. Used stole wraps and Cossack-styled capes for day and eveningwear.

Bonnie Cashin: The "Cashin look," comfortable country and travel clothes in wool jersey, knits, tweeds, canvas, and leather. Embraced ethnic fashions and fabrics of proven practicality—the toga cape; shell coat; sleeveless leather jerkin; poncho; long fringed, mohair, plaid at-home skirt; kimono coat piped in leather; hooded jersey dress; double-pocket handbag; soft knee-high boots; purse-pocket raincoat with interior pocket (to hold a purse); and sweater knits.

Oleg Cassini: Ultra-feminine styles—tiny waistlines and wide skirts in taffeta and chiffon; glamorous sheath dresses; knitted suits; and cocktail dresses.

Gabrielle "Coco" Chanel: Paris shop reopened in 1954, after closing at the start of WW II, with suits and sweater sets like those showed in the '30s.

Lilly Daché: Designed to outfit a woman from head to toe: tiny hats, dresses, coats, and low-heeled fabric shoes decorated with costume jewelry.

Christian Dior: Skirts 16 inches from the floor, and ankle length for late day. Featured chiffon sheath dresses with spaghetti straps and coolie hats, which were worn low and trimmed with bows. (Unfortunately, the term "coolie hat" now denotes the cone-shaped straw hats worn by Chinese laborers.) A collection of white handkerchief lawn jackets with soft pleats for evening and a line of V-shaped collars. Khaki bush jackets with flap pockets and tunic dresses in black, navy blue, and white.

Galanos: Uncompromising devotion to flawless construction and purity of line, one of the first designers to show horseshoe necklines on suits. Sheath and sack dresses had attached drapery for a fluid line. Lavish excess of chiffon (50 yards to a skirt), and layered cutaway collars.

Rudi Gernreich: Sportswear, casual clothing, and swimwear. Supple fabrics in solid and geometric patterns. Maillot-style swimsuit without inner foundation, in contrast to the highly constructed suits of the day, and bare suits with deeply cutout sides.

Hubert de Givenchy: The "Bettina" blouse, a peasant shape in shirting material with wide-open neck and full ruffled sleeves; elegant evening dresses and gowns; and sack-shaped dresses.

Claire McCardell: Practical clothes for the average working girl. Introduced details from men's clothing: large pockets, shirtwaist sleeves, stitching on blue jeans, and trouser pleats. Originated the "American look"—separates inspired by travel needs using sturdy cotton denims, ticking, gingham, and wool jersey. Credited with balloon bloomer playsuit; signature spaghetti belt; ballet slippers for streetwear; and the diaper-wrap one-piece swimsuit.

Rose Marie Reid: Swimsuits with conical bosoms.

THE '60s

It is hard to imagine a decade where culture and fashion went through greater change than the '60s—a veritable explosion of rebellion, emancipation, discovery, and political upheaval. These years broke with tradition to create the miniskirt, *Star Trek* tunic, bodysuit, hot pants, fringed suede, op and pop patterns, bell-bottom, paisley and psychedelic prints, tie-dyed looks, Vidal Sassoon haircuts, and a counterculture uniform of blue jeans, T-shirts, and long, unkempt hair.

The era launched unisex and ready-to-wear, dethroning the stylistic supremacy of Paris couture. Faith in technology and the future were evident in the vinyls and see-through plastics of Pierre Cardin and André Courrèges. Paco Rabanne experimented with chain mail and plastics. Zandra Rhodes was the rage, Levi Strauss the staple, and Emilio Pucci brought color and pattern. Clothes became body art. By the late '60s, even nudity began to gain public acceptance with topless swimwear, waitresses, nightclub dancers, and theater productions such as *Hair*.

From the sedate "shift" of the late '50s and early '60s, by the mid-'60s all bets were off. Women discovered the sexual emancipation of the Pill, mankind landed on the moon, the Beatles played in New York, and people discovered they really could have an effect on politics by protesting the war and other injustices.

For young men especially, the idea that they could wear striped bell-bottom trousers, long collared puffy-sleeved shirts, beaded and fringed suede vests, an assortment of beads and peace signs, and long hair was intoxicating.

With the emergence of mod, London's Mary Quant, and the mini, hemlines leapt from just below the knee to as short as possible. Quickly, stockings and garter belts became virtually obsolete, and with the advent of the circular sewing machine, seamed hose disappeared and pantyhose and patterned tights became an integral part of the look. With better fabrics available, the stiff, circular coned bra gave way to a more natural shape with the molded one-piece bra cup and the bra-less look emerged with the Women's Liberation movement.

The decade saw a lot of ethnic influences: the gypsy look, the gaucho look (complete with mid-calf culottes and gaucho hat), the Indian Nehru jacket, Moroccan-inspired caftans, and African dashikis as men and women discovered that "black is beautiful." After the success of *Dr. Zhivago*, Dior revived the

Russian look with fur-trimmed maxi coats and flat leather boots. In the '60s, Emilio Pucci, Karl Langerfeld, Balenciaga, Mary Quant, Jean Louis, and Valentino put their design talents to creating uniforms for (what were then known as) airhostesses—today a hot item on Internet auction sites.

Boots were made from bright colors, prints, and faux leopard; some reached above the knee to complement the ever-shortening skirts, and white mid-calf kid go-go boots made their debut. Jewelry was big, gold chain belts came into vogue, and earrings were of candelabra proportions. Fabrics were bright, patterns bold (think Goldie Hawn and Judy Carne in *Laugh In*), and often geometric.

Courrèges designed architecturally-inspired A-line dresses. Waistlines were raised to empire heights, dropped below the waist, or were ignored altogether in trapeze dresses and the baby doll look. Fashion models—from Britain's Twiggy, who embodied the mod look with her boyish haircut, big eyes rimmed with painted eyelashes, ultra thin, flat-chested figure, and gangling legs, to the tall, luscious Veruschka—became icons at opposite ends of the body spectrum.

MANUFACTURERS AND DESIGNERS TO LOOK FOR

Geoffrey Beene: Casual, comfortable, feminine clothes in the mood of Chanel, Cardin, and Norell. Cotton suits; black bias cut dresses; baby chemises; gambler's stripes; djellabas; and gypsy looks.

Bill Blass: Women's classic sportswear in men's fabrics: elegant mixtures of patterns, knits, tweeds, and shirtings coordinated with sweaters, hats, shoes, and hose. Glamorous eveningwear: lace, ruffles, and feathers. Furs, rainwear, watches, luggage, and scarves.

Pierre Cardin: Coats with draped hemlines and loose back panels; the envelope, barrel, and bubble skirts; chemises; minidresses; cartridge pleated wools with scalloped edges; irregular hems; and the first "nude" look. Metal body jewelry; unisex astronaut suits; helmets; bat wing jumpsuits; and tunics over tights.

Oleg Cassini: Official designer for Jacqueline Kennedy. Sleeveless high-waisted evening dress with a decorative single fabric rose, and a boxy-jacketed suit with fabric-covered buttons.

Ossie Clark: Metallic leather and snakeskin; revealing designs in satin jersey and chiffon with deep necklines.

Cole: "Scandal Suit" with cutout sides and deep V-shaped neckline plunged to the waist, cutouts filled with wide-mesh netting.

André Courrèges: Glorification of the very young—brief skirts, sculpted wools and knits, bold stripes, and dashing boots. His famed all white collection; above the knee dresses in crisp squared lines; suspender dresses in checked sequins or wide stripes; tunics over narrow pants with erotic seaming; white baby boots; industrial zippers; see-through dresses; cosmonaut suits; appliquéd flowers on the body and knee socks; knit cat-suits, and slit-eyed tennis ball sunglasses.

Oscar de la Renta: Russian and Gypsy fashion themes; belle époque fashions inspired by the paintings of Toulouse-Lautrec; transparent fabrics; swimwear; wedding dresses; sportswear; furs; and jewelry.

Rudi Gernreich: Topless swimsuit with straps that went over the shoulders and attached to the waist in front and back. "No-Brasuit" in skin-colored nylon net; clinging knit minidresses; "Swiss cheese" swimsuits; see-through blouses; knee-high leggings patterned to match tunic tops; and dhoti dresses.

Halston: Scarf hat; luxurious fur hats; both custom and ready-to-wear clothes; and scarves, furs, leather fashions, shoes, belts, jewelry, and wigs.

Norman Hartnell: Well-tailored suits and coats in wool and tweed; svelte daytime dresses; lavishly embroidered evening gowns.

Rene Lacoste: "Le Crocodile," short-sleeved knit polo shirts with a crocodile logo.

Karl Lagerfeld: Mole, rabbit, and squirrel fur coats and jackets dyed in bright colors; reversible fur coats; leather and fabric jackets.

Norman Norell: Culotte walking skirts; harem pants and pantsuits with tailored silhouettes; sequin-covered sheath dresses; and evening jumpsuits with calf-length knickers and sleeveless overcoats.

Emilio Pucci: A status symbol of the '60s, with brilliant heraldic prints on sheer jersey, and startling color combinations Clinging chemises; at-home robes; tights; signature scarves and dresses; resort shirts in designs from Sienese banners or with Sicilian or African motifs. 'Capsula' jumpsuit tapered to cover the feet with soft boots.

Lilly Pulitzer: Printed cotton shifts with ruffled hems and short sleeves; bikinis; print slacks for men; and "sneaky Pete" nightshirts.

Mary Quant: Turned London into "swinging" capital of the '60s. Designs were simple, aggressive, and emancipated, very "come on, look at me" colored tights, skinny ribs, hip belts, low slung hipster pants, no-bra bras, and miniskirts.

Yves Saint Laurent: Trapeze line; pea jacket; blazers; chemises divided into Mondrian-like blocks of bold colors; sportive leather; city pants; military jackets; see-through shirts and transparent dresses over nude body stockings; tuxedo jackets for women; and velvet knickers.

Scaasi: Simple gowns in aluminum colored cellophane or sheer silk and covered with huge sequins.

. . . .

THE '70S

The '70s were a decade of mixed messages, feminism, the Watergate scandal, antiwar and student movements, rock music, and youthful counterculture. Women abandoned conservative staples in favor of miniskirts, bright colors and patterns, and braless flowing caftans and tunics.

At the beginning of the decade, skirts were still amazingly short, to the point where dresses (sometimes called "sizzlers") had panties made of the same fabric, and all but the most conservative women were showing plenty of knee. Patterned hose and boots took on a new importance. Hot pants made a brief appearance, short shorts worn as daywear rather than sportswear. They were quickly rejected by women in the early '70s, and when Seventh Avenue introduced the mid-calf length midi skirt, many companies lost an entire season's income by mistaking what women wanted. Longer skirts slowly began to appear, usually with snaps in front which women opened to continue showing a large amount of leg.

Designers such as Bob Mackie took extreme glam designs for stars such as Elton John and Cher to new heights, letting imagination, ethnic influences, and outrageous concepts take them where few had gone before. Performers' shoes sometimes had platforms seven or eight inches high, decorated with rhinestones and sequins. Television shows such as *Charlie's Angels* and *Wonder Woman* set style examples for the '70s woman. Toward the end of the decade, *Saturday Night Fever* heavily influenced the way people dressed as they danced to popular disco music. John Travolta's three-piece white polyester suit created a lasting image that still epitomizes what we think of as disco today.

Nylon shirts and polyester suits for men were forward-looking by virtue of fiber, but their flared bell-bottoms and wide lapels were romantic, foppish, and nostalgic. Much of peasant/exotic/hippie fashion found its way into mass market ready-to-wear design, and men's fashions often matched women's in bright colors, loud patterns, and styles that pushed the envelope. Men's hairdos and sideburns were long, and women's hair was often waist length and straight (women set their hair with empty beer cans, the only "rollers" big enough to create the Cher look!).

"Granny" dresses, "prairie" blouses, and patchwork skirts were very popular in the early '70s and were often paired with blouses made of a cheese-cloth fabric or cotton. Caftans were worn in everything from Indian cotton prints, imported Moroccan styles, and more expensive satins and brocades for evening. In Los Angeles, there were even "caftan parties" with men and women arriving fully adorned in caftans!

Yves Saint Laurent and Kenzo, a new talent from Japan, set the tone in Paris with bohemian, gypsy, and ethnic looks. Fashion capitals expanded from Paris and New York to Milan and Tokyo with Takada Kenzo, Missoni, Comme des Garçons by Rei Kawakuba, Emilio Pucci, and Giorgio Armani, a menswear designer, who led the Milanese into prominence with deconstructed pantsuits for women.

In 1972, the Nike brand made its debut, and athleticwear became fashionable. Sportswear, T-shirts, and sweatshirts went out at night, and women wore T-shirts with wrap skirts and pants to the office. Leotards appeared outside dance class.

Status dressing dictated that even the humble blue jean could acquire "designer" cachet. Denim was embroidered, patched, appliquéd, and worn so tight that it was not uncommon for women to have to lie flat on their backs to get their jeans zipped up! Some wore a new pair into the bathtub to have them shrink to their body's shape.

Today, 1970s fashions are abundant in vintage stores all over the United States and Canada. Look for bell-bottoms, angel-sleeved blouses, bamboo purses, shirts with long collars, earth shoes, mood rings, caftans, patchwork skirts, granny gowns, platform boots, polyester leisure suits, puka shells, satin baseball jackets, and disco dresses.

MANUFACTURERS AND DESIGNERS TO LOOK FOR

Laura Ashley: Fabrics with floral motifs. Edwardian style of high collars and leg-of-mutton sleeves.

Stephan Burrows: At-home leisure clothes; matte jersey disco fashions; top stitching in contrasting colors; uneven hemlines; multiple layering of chiffon; leather decorated with studded nails; lettuce-edged skirts; and suede hot pants.

André Courrèges: Feminine collection using ruffles, and softer colors and fabrics. Full, floor-length skirts scattered with appliquéd flowers, and tight high-waisted bodices.

Diane von Furstenberg: Combined simplistic elegance, practicality, and comfort in mid-length wrap dresses with long sleeves and closely fitted tops in geometric and floral printed jersey.

Gucci: Accessories, namely purses and scarves.

Halston: Sweaters; wide-leg pants and turtlenecks; simple clothing that clings to the body; and tie-dyed fabrics.

Betsey Johnson: Stretchy designs of matte jersey for disco dancing; brightly colored knits; hip-hugger pants; princess line dresses; swimwear, retro sundresses, and off-the-shoulder tops with leggings.

Norma Kamali: Quilted coats of nylon and down; sweatshirt material for pants, jackets, shirts, and short cheerleader skirts; suits, silk dresses, and wrap-style swimwear.

Takada Kenzo: With clothes that blend east and west, herevolutionized the art of modern dressing. Menswear was a hybrid of Western tailoring and Eastern sarongs, while women's clothing combined Japanese cuts with Slavic embroidery. Full, deep kimono-style sleeves and squared shoulders in a knitwear collection of separates and shawls. Hooded sweaters in boucle knit that looked like Persian lamb; the trapunto stitched look; reversible blousons; and fabric sweater with knit cuffs and waistband.

Calvin Klein: Clean silhouette, refined color, and natural fibers. Sweaters, pants, skirts, dresses, shirts, coats, and capes.

Mary McFadden: Clothes in Eastern silks; Japanese and American hand-painted silk batiks cut to move with the body. Indonesian fabrics for jackets with removable fur linings. Fabrics quilted vertically to keep them narrow and skinny, or with outline stitching to make them look rounder and more voluptuous.

Zandra Rhodes: Unevenly hemmed chiffon gowns, quilted tunics, and embroidered satins. Imaginative hand-screened prints on soft fabrics; art deco motifs; soft butterfly dresses; and slit-side chiffons with edges cut by pinking shears.

Yves Saint Laurent: Soft refined clothing; pleated shirtdresses; long-jacket suits; backless evening dresses, and "Le Smoking" tuxedo jackets. Menswear line of suits, sportswear, outerwear, sweaters, and shirts.

Giorgio di Sant'Angelo: Leotards, bodysuits, and dresses with wrap skits in stretchy jersey with bright, bold-patterned prints. Western Navaho and gypsy-inspired designs.

It hardly seems that enough time has passed for styles from the 1980s to be considered vintage or collectible, but what goes around comes around, and coming around it is!

As one popular saying put it, "whoever dies with the most toys, wins." *Wall Street* film character Gordon Gekko told us "greed is good," while the trickle-down financial policies of Ronald Reagan and Margaret Thatcher encouraged a "shop till you drop" mentality of spend, spend, spend that was portrayed as almost patriotic. The '80s were epitomized by what was known as "the me decade," portrayed in the entertainment media to perfection with TV's *Dynasty* and *Dallas* and their fascination with big money, power, glitz, and glamour. Costume designer Nolan Miller's dresses and suits with huge shoulder pads for stars Lynda Evans and Joan Collins became the look to emulate. Worn even with the lowliest of T-shirts to magnify what padding the manufacturers had already put in, shoulder pads were so de riguer that every woman had her favorite pair to tuck under her bra straps.

It was the decade of the Yuppie (the young urban professional) the power suit, and the pursuit of riches. For women, suits were very popular, with wide shoulders, nipped waists, and slim short skirts. Colors were bright. Turquoise, red, apple green, fuschia, and purple were the colors of the day, although women in business tended to wear their suits in darker colors. Lapels often had added trim or contrasting edging, and dresses had beading, sequins, large stones, gold studs, and appliqués to add pizzazz. And to balance it all—big hair!

Jewelry was also enormous, usually gold for daytime, with huge hoops, buttons, and dangles achieving astounding proportions—evening earrings touched the shoulders. Long gold chains with intermittent pearls or colored glass beads were popular, as were large brooches to adorn lapels of suits and coatdresses.

Eveningwear was also colorful and elaborate and very, very glitzy! Ball gowns had huge satin skirts, or were beaded from top to bottom.

Costume and fashion designer Bob Mackie's gowns for Ann-Margret and Cher said "glamour" like no one else's, and his beaded gowns adorned every female star in Hollywood.

Power dressing was a high maintenance, ultra-groomed look, and makeup became heavier and more dramatic. Big, regularly coiffured hair and carefully manicured feet and nails testified to the possession of lots of disposable income.

The 1980s were also the decade when designers proudly displayed their initials or logo on their products, and men and women were proud to carry these new status symbols. GG and LV (Gucci and Louis Vuitton) were everywhere, and soon we were all sporting initials, logos, and even complete designer names across our chests or backs.

The fitness craze was in full form in the '80s, and gear formerly reserved for the gym made its way into the streets and malls of America. With the improvement of stretch fabrics, leggings became hot property and worn with oversize blouses and sneakers as everyday wear. Sweat suits became part of the mainstream wardrobe in everything from basic gray to colorful velour. Inspired by *Flashdance* fashions by costume designer Michael Kaplan, who was originally inspired by a dancer's need to keep their muscles warm, leg warmers in every color and style became de rigeur. Raquel Welch even wore sequin leg warmers in her Las Vegas nightclub act!

Other influences were music videos, which pushed the envelope in terms of visual images. Madonna, Boy George, and Annie Lennox all expressed themselves in unique and daring ways.

Wedding fashion seesawed from one extreme to another; from softly romantic to body-hugging showgirl sheaths with overtrain. Although she later publicly admitted that perhaps her gown was a bit over the top, Princess Diana's choice for her 1981 marriage to Prince Charles was reflective of the times. The sleeves on her ivory silk taffeta gown were as large as her head. Eventually through the decade, the shoulder softened into a rounded, rather than squared, silhouette—but was still exaggerated.

Adolfo: Quiet, classic style. His first client was Gloria Vanderbilt and his most famous Nancy Reagan, for whom he made a red wool inauguration coat and matching braided toque.

Azzedine Alaïa: Figure-hugging dresses in leather, cashmere, and stretch fabrics.

Giorgio Armani: Suits and jackets—wide-shouldered look for executive women.

Laura Ashley: Puffed sleeves, smocks, and voluminous dresses with patch pockets available in a variety of pretty cotton prints, including stripes, dots, and floral springs; cotton summer dresses that evoke thoughts of garden parties; and cable-knit sweaters prompting memories of long weekends spent in the country.

Benetton: Colorful casual wear and knitwear separates.

Hugo Boss: Suits worn by characters in the primetime television series *Dallas* and *L.A. Law.*

Perry Ellis: Sportswear in clean lines, crisp fabrics—a cross between lounging and activity. His easy-to-wear slouch look consisted of loose trousers, layered tunics, and oversized sweaters.

Comme des Garçons: Label formed by designer Rei Kawakubo. Muted colors and a radical approach to cutting and shaping.

Oscar de la Renta: Signature is flamboyance and color. He was the first American designer to head a Parisian couture house. Famous for opulent eveningwear, that is both vibrant and tasteful. Clients include Liza Minnelli, Nancy Reagan, Joan Collins, Ivana Trump, Jacqueline Onassis, and Faye Dunaway.

John Galliano: Innovative and quirky styles, popular with the younger buyer.

Jean Paul Gaultier: Slashed and layered look.

Herbert de Givenchy: The man who helped make Audrey Hepburn an icon of elegance. "All a woman needs to be chic are a raincoat, two suits, a pair of trousers, and a cashmere sweater," said Givenchy, as reported by *Vogue.*

Hermès: Top quality, bold, colorfully printed scarves.

Norma Kamali: Fashionable sportswear, including a "sweats" collection and officewear for the executive woman. Hers was an innovative approach to fabric with possibly the largest shoulder pads to be seen.

Donna Karan: Donna Karan New York (DKNY) launched the first Donna Karan collection. Sticking to her fashion philosophy of designing clothes she would like to wear, Karan developed a line of clothing that was basic, functional, and eminently wearable. Karan's comfortable wrap skirts, khaki trench coats, and her famous "bodysuits" flew off the shelves—one major Fifth Avenue store sold its entire DKNY stock in just one afternoon!

Takado Kenzo: Paved the way for the wider popularity of Japanese designers in the '70s and '80s, known for his successful blend of Eastern and Western styles.

Calvin Klein: Smooth, understated look; shirtwaists.

Christian Lacroix: Big, showy, fitted evening gowns, flaring at the hem like a flamenco dancer or swelling with petticoats of alarming proportions. Out and out puffballs or poufs, with fitted corset tops, rustling taffetas, and shimmering silks decorated with bows, flounces, ruffles, and bustles. Extraordinary and daring use of color.

Karl Lagerfeld: Imaginative and witty designs; revived the miniskirt by taking the traditional mid-calf length Chanel skirt and slashing the hem, creating the micro-mini suit. Used electric pink and lime green tartan tweeds, along with denim and leather, pearls the size of golf balls, and shiny, brash gold chains.

Ralph Lauren: Quality fabrics for men and women, designer for the "Yuppie" buyer, "frontier fashion" collection.

Bob Mackie: Translated his successful glamour look for performers into a couture line of evening gowns that often featured built-in bras, asymmetrical draping at the hip, and elaborate beading. He became known in the U.S. first for his work with comedienne Carol Burnett; he was responsible for her on-set wardrobe.

Nolan Miller: After his success with designs for Linda Evans, Joan Collins, and TV's primetime soap *Dynasty*, he launched his own line of wide-shouldered suits, cocktail dresses, and eveningwear.

Claude Montana: "Power dressing," generous and square-cut shoulder pads.

Issey Miyake: Bold cutting, draping, and innovative use of textures and sculptural shapes.

Thierry Mugler: Proponent of the hour-glass and figure-hugging fashions of the '80s, although styles were often influenced by fashions of the '40s and '50s.

Yves Saint Laurent: Short skirts, leather garments, and cinched waists.

Emanuel Ungaro: Sizzling color, feminine shapes, and wildflowers are his signature. Celebrity clients include French actress Anouk Aimée and Texas socialite Lynn Wyatt.

Gianni Versace: In 1982, this Italian designer exploded onto the fashion scene, dazzling the world with sexy chain mail dresses. In the late '80s, Gianni brought his sister Donatella on board—to play the role of muse. But Donatella soon became Gianni's co-designer, launching the Versace diffusion line Versus in 1989.

Vivienne Westwood: Showed her first collection, Pirate, in London. The show put her firmly on the fashion map as an original and unusual design talent. Her uncompromising and often provocative designs continue to hit the headlines, securing a global audience for her clothes. Early '80s pieces can be identified by any of the following labels: Sex original; 430 King's Road; Malcolm McClaren, Vivienne Westwood, Seditionaires, and World's End, McClaren, Weedwood, born in England.

Yohji Yamamoto: Loose, unstructured, but cleverly cut black and white garments. In the late '80s, he began to allow color to appear in his collections.

LOS ANGELES

LOS ANGELES

Hollywood is the birthplace of glamour, from the blond bombshells of yesteryear to the glittering stars on today's red carpets. It epitomizes style, elegance, and sophistication, and nowhere is this more apparent than in the city's vintage and resale market.

The city's abundance of celebrities keep the high-end resale stores packed with beautiful garments. Many actresses wear stunning designer gowns to events, are photographed for *People* or *InStyle* magazine, and then immediately turn the dresses into their favorite resale shop. Most resale stores are very discreet about keeping the identity of these celebrities private, but Faye Dunaway, for one, allows her name to be used on the price tags of her cast-off Armani's. Finding a Pamela Dennis or Valentino gown in pristine condition for a mere 10 to 30 percent of its original price is a dream that can come true in Los Angeles.

Celebrities also demand vintage, preferring items that give them an original look that's definitely NOT from the mall. From a perfectly preserved gown worn by a 1940s film star to funky and eclectic items rediscovered in some-one's attic, Los Angeles is home to a wide range of excellent vintage stores.

In addition, Los Angeles is the only city in the world (that we know of) that has several stores that sell nothing but wardrobe from the studios, canceled television series, and completed films. These pieces, for the most part, have been worn by an actor in only one or two scenes, perhaps over the course of a few days (weeks at the most), dry cleaned, and then made available for resale.

Other costume designers involved in costuming period films such as *Pearl Harbor* or *Titanic*, shop in vintage stores for the period clothes they need—for both the principal actors and sometimes hundreds of extras. Where else will they find five hundred 1940s men's suits and fedoras? And eventually these things make their way back into the market!

SO JOIN IN THE FUN AND LET'S SHOP ...

AAARDVARK'S ODD ARK

$

7579 Melrose Ave., Los Angeles 90046; (323) 655-6769.
Open Sun–Thurs: noon–8 p.m., Fri/Sat: 11 a.m.–9 p.m.

> *Owner:* Joe Stromei
> *Return Policy:* All sales final
> *Try-on Facilities:* Dressing rooms with outside mirrors

Aaardvark's Odd Ark is a struggling actor's or designer's heaven, a very eclectic mix of the best-worst-old-funky-horrible-wonderful clothes and costumes from the 1920s–80s. "We specialize in lower priced clothes," says Stromei, "as the store is very busy and we can't take care of very fine, expensive, fragile pieces." The better, rarer pieces are displayed on the wall, and include rare kimonos, Victorian pieces, and Hawaiian shirts.

With simple, homey décor—to avoid distracting customers from the clothes—this store has it all: casual and semi-casual, semi-formal and formal, clubwear, streetwear for men and women, new and used jeans, cords, camo pants, ties, overalls, jumpsuits, guayaberas, dashikis, petticoats, feather boas, furry coats, velvet jackets, halter tops, party wigs, work clothes, dresses, Hawaiian shirts, tie-dye, lingerie, ties, bow ties, hats, scarves, belts, and cufflinks.

Also at 85 Market St., Venice 90291; (310) 392-2996.
1253 E. Colorado Blvd., Pasadena 91106; (626) 583-9109.

ALICE AND ANNIE

$$

11056 Magnolia Blvd., North Hollywood 91601; (818) 761-6085.
Open Tues–Thurs and Sat: noon–6 p.m., Fri: noon–8 p.m.

Owner: Alice and Annie Ahbur
Return Policy: Exchange only
Try-on Facilities: One dressing room with mirror

Alice and Annie is run by a mother-and-daughter team and is located in North Hollywood within an area called "NoHo." Entering their small store is like walking into a Victorian secret garden complete with trellis, silk flowers, lots of lace, fringed lamps, antique armoires, and stacks of antique hatboxes (some of which are for sale). Annie and her associates obviously care passionately about their clothes, as evidenced by many of the older pieces carefully hung on padded hangers. They have beautiful Victorian blouses, '20s pieces (one spectacular black beaded dress), plus lots of '30s, '40s, and '50s items, mostly for women. Day dresses from this era are in good condition, and the owners stress that they make a point of finding larger sizes for today's "healthier" woman. Other specialties are beautiful lingerie, '20s beaded evening purses, and '50s Lucite bags. The Ahburs love Hedda Hopper hats and Gloria Swanson lingerie. Their favorite periods are the 1920s–40s for glamorous evening wear. It comes as no surprise that both Patricia Arquette and Daryl Hannah have reportedly shopped here.

AMERICAN RAG COMPAGNIE
$$

150 S. La Brea Ave., Los Angeles 90036; (323) 935-3154.
Open Mon–Sat: 10 a.m.–9 p.m., Sun: noon–7 p.m.
www.AmRag.com

Owner: Mark and Margot Werts
Return Policy: All sales final
Try-on Facilities: One dressing room with mirror

American Rag Compagnie carries upscale vintage and is very fashion oriented, with additional boutiques in Japan (thus their "Tokyo" influence) and San Francisco. The Werts personally collect 1940s Salvadore Dali ties. Their favorite fashion decade? "Whatever's in fashion today because vintage is

NOT dress up, it is an ACTUAL way of dressing." Their stock, which originated in Europe and the United States, is extensive—currently 25,000 units in stores and one million units in their warehouse.

City Rags
$

10967 Weyburn Ave., Los Angeles 90024; (310) 209-0889.
Open Sun–Thurs: 11:30 a.m.–8 p.m., Fri/Sat: 11:30 a.m.–10 p.m.

Owner: Philippe and Denise Badreau
Return Policy: All sales final
Try-on Facilities: One dressing room with mirrors

City Rags' husband-and-wife-team, Denise and Philippe, recognized a serious need for a retail facelift in UCLA-adjacent Westwood Village, and City Rags was born. This boutique offers Melrose Avenue-attitude vintage clothes at a fraction of the price. Merchandise from the 1960s–80s includes sportswear, Levi's bell-bottoms, vintage T-shirts, denim jackets, poly shirts and pants, corduroy pants, and leather jackets. Easy to navigate, this boutique separates vintage jeans by style—bell-bottoms to your left, '80s straight legs to your right, and '70s straight legs down the middle. Denise has an eye for faux fur chubbies, T-shirts with funky iron-ons, and shearling-lined jackets, while Philippe locates polyester button-downs with wild and wearable patterns.

Can't find what you're looking for? All you need to do is ask—Denise and Philippe will do their best to hunt it down.

Decades, Inc.
$$$

8214 Melrose Ave. (upstairs), Los Angeles 90046; (323) 655-0223.
Open Mon–Sat: 11:30 a.m.–6 p.m. or by appointment.
www.DecadesInc.com

Owner: Cameron Silver
Return Policy: All sales final
Try-on Facilities: Dressing room the size of most Hong Kong apartments, private with a three-way mirror

Decades, Inc. specializes in 1960s–70s vintage couture that looks modern—a mix of primitive luxury and mid-century design. The store resembles a cross between Warhol's factory and Kubrick's *2001* spacecraft. This shop, a gold mine of '60s and '70s fashions, is stocked with influential modern designers of yesteryear, including Courrèges, Hermès, Gucci, Gernreich, Rabánne, Koos van den Akker, and Halston. "We have the largest collection of Ossie Clark—who continues to be a very influential designer. We also have the Loris Azzaro archives, which are incredibly sexy and includes jersey dresses and metallic Lurex knits," says Silver. "The '60s and '70s—the birth of modern fashion—continue to be copied by contemporary designers season after season."

They have the YSL Rive Gauche collection of Madame de Revill (director of Rive Gauche from 1968–95) numbering over 300 pieces. Look for Hermès '60s and '70s handbags, jewelry, and ready-to-wear classics as well as a plethora of men's vintage designer clothing from Cardin, North Beach Leather, and Nudie's (a famous Western wear store). You've seen their clothes on the big screen in F*ight Club, Legally Blond, The Mexican,* and *Planet of the Apes.*

Decades, Inc. also carries "remodeled" vintage clothing and jewelry. Each piece is one-of-a-kind, ethnic, and '70s inspired. We are told that Sandra Bullock wore one of the bead and feather lariats to an awards show. Silver's personal collection includes a Madame Grés sample gown from the '60s. Celebrities who reportedly shop this boutique include Téa Leoni, Brad Pitt, Kirstie Alley, Cameron Diaz, Courtney Love, Marilyn Manson, David Arquette, Rose McGowan, and Jennifer Tilly.

"The trick is to make vintage an integral part of your style. If you wear vintage for vintage's sake, people will look at your outfit, not at you."
—ROBERT TURTURICE, EMMY-WINNER FOR COSTUME DESIGN IN *MOONLIGHTING*

GOLYESTER

$$

136 S. La Brea Ave., Los Angeles 90036; (323) 931-1339.
Open Mon–Sat: 11 a.m.–6 p.m.

Owner: Ester Ginsberg
Return Policy: All sales final
Try-on Facilities: Private dressing room with mirror

Golyester has been in business for over 20 years. Ginsberg carved her niche in the vintage marketplace with her selection of embroidered shawls, Chinese robes, and unusual, opulent pieces. Her personal treasures include a Chinese shawl embroidered with hundreds of people, animals, and insects; and a Victorian smoking jacket made of cigar labels from her AD RAGS™ collection. Featured in the *Los Angeles Times Sunday Magazine* for their knockout window displays by Linda Davies, Golyster stocks the best vintage clothing and textiles from the 1900s–1960s. Her favorite? Pre '50s, "when clothing was beautifully sewn and detailed and outrageously over-the-top with humorous designs."

HIDDEN TREASURES

$$

154 Topanga Canyon Blvd., Los Angeles 90290; (310) 455-2998.
Open Daily: 10:30 a.m.–6:30 p.m.

Owner: Darrell Hazen
Return Policy: Next day return
Try-on Facilities: Three dressing rooms with mirrors

Hidden Treasures owner Darrell Hazen combs the Midwest for vintage clothing because of the history and stories surrounding each piece. Shoppers will find the dates these treasures were born written right on the price tags. Hazen transports shoppers back to the 1920s (with beaded dresses) and the 1930s (with simple floor-length rayon dresses). An 1890s violet velvet opera cape with metallic gold thread and mother of pearl binoculars tops his personal collection.

HUBBA HUBBA!
$$

3220 W. Magnolia Blvd., Burbank 91505; (818) 845-0636.
Open Tues–Sat: noon–6 p.m.

Owner: Patricia Taylor
Return Policy: Exchange with receipt
Try-on Facilities: One large room with mirrors

Hubba Hubba! is so jam-packed with 1930s–60s vintage that there's no room for décor. Taylor stocks at least 100 new pieces in the store every week. "Not only do costume designers frequent my shop year after year when they're working on period TV, film, and theater projects, but there's a treasure chest of great stuff for singers, actors, and anyone who doesn't want to look like everyone else. Vintage is so much more interesting, stylish, and well-made than current fashion," says Taylor.

Loads of costume jewelry—glitzy rhinestone, glass beads, and sterling pieces—are for sale. Check out their shoe room for shoes, a zillion hats, and purses. Peruse their lovely vintage wedding gowns, prom gowns, vintage rayon robes, dresses, and men's suits and shirts. Taylor carries it all, but her favorite decade is the '40s for the "classy, great lines and figure flattering clothes—I like that period on the guys, too!"

Taylor's stock comes from "pickers" and estate sales around the country. She takes pride in offering such reasonable prices that "high-end dealers can buy here and still double the price." In the 17 years that this store has been in Burbank, it has helped wardrobe hundreds of films, including *Pearl Harbor.*

IGUANA VINTAGE CLOTHING

$

14422 Ventura Blvd., Los Angeles 91423; (818) 907-6716.
Open Mon–Thurs: 11 a.m.–7 p.m., Fri/Sat: 11 a.m.–8 p.m.,
Sun: 11 a.m.–6 p.m.
www.IguanaClothing.com

Owner:	Sheila Cohn
Return Policy:	All sales final
Try-on Facilities:	Six changing rooms on first floor, two on mezzanine; full-length mirrors located outside dressing rooms and throughout the store

Iguana Vintage Clothing looks like a clean, well-organized Western store and offers vintage clothing from the 1920s–80s, including leather jackets, '60s miniskirts, zoot suits, top hats, poodle skirts, bell-bottoms, wedding gowns, platform shoes, flapper dresses, cowboy and biker boots, saddle shoes, bowling shirts, '40s and '50s dress suits, cashmere sweaters, trench coats, leather vests, and Hawaiian and paisley shirts. Whew! And accessories!

Cohn's favorite era is the '40s. "The clothes were fun yet very stylish, the material very comfortable—especially anything in gabardine," says Cohn. She loves men in fedora hats, suspenders, and two-tone shoes, and for the ladies, free flowing dresses with or without pleats. Her personal collection boasts first edition 501 Levi's in perfect condition and color.

"Buy one really good suit, one really good coat, and add trendy accessories. Accessories change with the season, but a classic look stays and stays."
—GIOVANNA OTTOBRE-MELTON, COSTUME DESIGNER FOR *PROVIDENCE*

IT'S A WRAP!
PRODUCTION WARDROBE SALES

$$

3315 W. Magnolia Blvd., Burbank 91505; (818) 567-7366.
Open Mon–Fri: 11 a.m.–8 p.m., Sat/Sun: 11 a.m.–6 p.m.
www.ItsAWrapHollywood.com

Owner: Tiara Nappi and Jan Dion
Return Policy: All sales final
Try-on Facilities: Nine dressing rooms

It's A Wrap! Production Wardrobe Sales looks like a combination of a movie set and museum and specializes in wardrobe from the sets of film and TV. Jan Dion, self-proclaimed founder of the concept of selling production wardrobe, came up with the idea over 17 years ago during a directors strike. Dion was asked to auction off props and equipment from *Raise the Titanic, The Muppet Movie,* and *Hard Country* to raise money. Entire wardrobe trailers were sold for pennies on the dollar, but the auction inspired her. So Dion opened a small store in Studio City to sell items from the movies to the public.

Dion ran her shop, Retake Room, for ten years before she and her daughter, Tiara Nappi, opened It's a Wrap!, named for the phrase that signifies the end of a film shoot. Today they have a 7,000-square-foot showroom with 3,000 square feet of storage.

The front showroom holds contemporary wardrobe for men and women, while the back showroom offers contemporary, vintage, and costume clothing. The stock varies depending on the featured movie or television show. Each item is tagged according to the movie, TV show, commercial, or runway on which it appeared. Some of the clothing has never been worn, the rest is dry cleaned.

Occasionally the wardrobe has been "teched" or "distressed" for a particular scene. "Teching" means dying a white garment a light tan or gray to reduce glare on camera; "distressing" means anything from making a garment look old and worn to creating knife tears, bullet holes, or fake blood splatters. These items are more likely to end up on the wall for display only.

In their showroom, prices are reduced directly on the store tag every three weeks. Current offerings include: a *Charmed* floral silk blouse worn by a cast member; an *Autumn in New York* cream satin gown worn by Winona Ryder; and a *Xena: Warrior Princess* costume worn by Lucy Lawless. Resale pieces include Donna Karan, Dolce & Gabbana, Lanvin, Prada, Gucci, Escada, BCBG, and Betsy Johnson. The most interesting pieces collected by Nappi are from Winona Ryder's wardrobe for *Autumn in New York*.

JET RAG

$

825 N. La Brea Ave., Los Angeles 90038; (323) 939-0528.
Open Mon–Sat: 11:30 a.m.–8 p.m., Sun: 11 a.m.–7:30 p.m.

> **Owner:** Jimba Kobayashi
> **Return Policy:** All sales final
> **Try-on Facilities:** Five dressing rooms

Jet Rag, one of the best sources for well-priced vintage clothing, is a post-apocalyptic store housed in an imposing rust colored building on trendy La Brea Avenue. Judging by the pierced salespeople and blasting music, young shoppers are their targeted customer. They offer a remarkably large and diversified collection of pants, tops, sweaters, leather and suede jackets, sleepwear, and gowns. The store is well-organized and easy to find, with most items in good condition, and all at very accessible prices.

Jet Rag offers an equal amount of men's and women's clothing, with most items from the '50s and forward. On Sundays, this store offers grab bag pieces for $1 each, but a good eye is a must to find something worthwhile, and a quick draw to grab it first.

Koboyasha has always been interested in vintage clothes; his store is your typical case of a hobby turning into a business. "Since new clothing floods the market with virtually the same thing everywhere you go," he tells us, "vintage clothing is a refreshing alternative because every single piece is different." As a collector, Koboyasha's personal favorite is split between a shirt by Elsa Schiaparelli famed for her surrealist fashions and a beautiful 1936 fur evening coat. His favorite era is the '50s. "It was the last decade in which silk, rayon, and wool were used very well. It also represents good times in America, from simple to wild and fun."

MEOW

$$

2210 E. Fourth St., Long Beach 90814; (562) 438-8990.
Open Tues–Sat: noon–6 p.m., Sun/Mon: noon–5 p.m.

> **Owner:** Kathleen Schaaf
> **Return Policy:** All sales final
> **Try-on Facilities:** Pink fridge doors that open to three mint and turquoise dressing rooms

Meow is an 1,800-square-foot oasis filled with mint-condition vintage, old neon signs, vintage advertisements, and an array of period mannequins. The store specializes in never worn originals from 1940s–70s, including apparel, accessories, sweaters, sweaters, and more sweaters. Cashmere sweaters from the '50s and '60s, cardigans, angora, mohair—200–300 sweaters are stocked, each lovingly hand-laundered before being put on display.

Count on Schaaf to have a terrific selection of handmade, never worn original sweaters that make up about 40 percent of their stock. "It's amazing that in 2002 I can still go out and find merchandise that has never been used from the 1940s–70s. It's like a treasure hunt. I never know what I'll find," says Schaaf. Her personal collection includes display and advertising related clothes, workwear, and denim sneakers from the '30s and '40s. Workwear and playclothes from the '40s are her favorite, though she loves '70s and '80s punk rock and new wave T-shirts—we found a never worn Led Zepplin T-shirt from the '70s ready for the taking.

Meow has supplied wardrobe for more films and TV shows than can be counted on both hands, including *Pleasantville*; *Austin Powers I* and *II*; *Detroit Rock City*; *Mulholland Falls*; *A Walk in the Clouds*; *Girl, Interrupted*; *Charlie's Angels*; *Liberty Heights*; *Remember the Titans*; *Thirteen Days*; *The Legend of Bagger Vance*; *The Drew Carey Show*; and *A League of Their Own*.

MOMO
$$

308 N. Stanley Ave., Los Angeles 90036; (323) 964-5240.
Open Mon/Tues and Thurs–Sat: noon–8 p.m., Sun: noon–6 p.m.

> *Owner:* Rie Fujii
> *Return Policy:* All sales final
> *Try-on Facilities:* Dressing room with mirror

Momo is Shabon's (see p. 66) "sister store" and specializes in '60s and '70s clothing and accessories, all of which are never worn or are in excellent condition. This store offers T-shirts, bell-bottoms, dresses, skirts, leather jackets, shoes, hats, and purses. Japanese in flavor, you will find, according to Fujii, "Astro Boy products, cool watches from Japan, and T-shirts with silk-screened work by Amore, a Tokyo-based artist whose imagry and humor are responsible for Momo's look."

Owner Fujii's personal collection includes H. Barc dead stock—shirts and pants that had been sitting in a warehouse for 30 years. Current offerings include: low-waisted bell-bottoms; airline bags by World Airwaves, Pan Am, United Airlines, and Sunair; as well as concert T-shirts and jerseys from bands such as Iron Maiden, Yes, Bon Jovi, the Who, Rolling Stones, Triumph, and Jefferson Starship.

Tara Reid was spotted at the 2002 Race to Erase MS in Los Angeles in a crocheted vintage granny gown.

OZZIE DOTS

$$

4637 Hollywood Blvd., Los Angeles 90027; (323) 663-2867.
Open Mon–Sat: 11 a.m.–6 p.m., Sun: noon–5 p.m.
www.OzzieDots.com

> *Owner:* Daniel Hazen
> *Return Policy:* All sales final
> *Try-on Facilities:* Four dressing rooms with three full-length mirrors

Ozzie Dots, decorated in festive and funky Polynesian, specializes in '40s and '50s glamour and glitz. "We specialize in vintage clothing and costumes, and we cater to the movie industry. Celebrities shop us. We are considered the one-stop shop in Los Angeles where treasures are to be found," says Hazen. Although primarily a vintage clothing boutique, Hazen does offer designer resale, including Dior, Ralph Lauren, Lilli Ann, Hermès, and Vera Wang. His favorite era is the '40s, "because of all the great prints, wonderful rayons, and beautiful designs."

A recent visit turned up a cream tuxedo jacket made for Lou Rawls, a fancy Western shirt by Turk, a Tuxedo shirt made for Dean Martin, and two dresses worn by Tatum O'Neal in *Paper Moon*. Wardrobe from Ozzie Dots appeared in *Annie Hall, Great Balls of Fire!*, and *Pleasantville*.

THE PAPER BAG PRINCESS

$$$

8700 Santa Monica Blvd., Los Angeles 90069; (310) 358-1985.
Open Mon–Sat: noon–7 p.m., Sun: noon–5 p.m.
www.ThePaperBagPrincess.com

> *Owner:* Elizabeth M. Mason
> *Return Policy:* All sales final
> *Try-on Facilities:* Dressing rooms with mirrors

The Paper Bag Princess first opened in 1995 in less than 300 square feet. Today there are three separate boutiques in over 3,000 square feet of space. The front store is women's vintage, contemporary garments, and accessories, while directly behind is the men's department. Specializing in sleek '60s and '70s styles, this store offers the "largest collection in the world of vintage Emilio Pucci clothing and vintage designs by Chanel, Hermès, Gucci, Cardin, Dior, Gernreich, Balenciaga, Yves Saint Laurent, and many others," says Mason.

In its September 1999 issue, *Los Angeles Magazine* lauded the exceptional quality of vintage clothing at the Paper Bag Princess. Many of Mason's vintage items have come from the closets of celebrities, giving the items a pedigree one may not find elsewhere. Courtney Love, Elizabeth Shue, Tori Spelling and Nicole Kidman are some of the stars that have been known to peruse the racks here, along with designers (Mason won't reveal who) who scour the store for inspiration.

Splendid finds might include: a YSL red shearling and black suede purse and muff; a black velvet wide-brim bolero hat with multi-colored dangling hearts; a black long-sleeved "furry" knit minidress; Chanel Number 5 rhinestone drop earrings; or black Alaïa knit capris.

PARIS 1900

$$$

2703 Main St., Santa Monica 90405; (310) 396-0405.
Open Mon–Sat by appointment or by chance.

    Owner: Susan Lieberman
  Return Policy: Exchange only
Try-on Facilities: One dressing room with mirror

The **Paris 1900** adventure begins at the front door with an Art Nouveau façade that was entirely handcrafted in 1981 by Parke Meek and Roger Johnson (inspired by an 1895 Paul Hankar Brussels façade). This store specializes in authentic fashion and bridal attire dating from 1900–1930, a period known for exquisite handwork. Newly designed garments using antique laces and textiles are also for sale. Each garment in this store is carefully selected based on quality and condition, restored, hand laundered, air dried, and pressed.

The Edwardian period and the '20s are Leiberman's favorites because of the wonderfully feminine detailing. Lieberman collects hand-embroidered pieces by Boué Soeurs and garments from the estate of May Rindge, founder of Malibu Pottery (1920s) and matriarch of family land holdings from Malibu to the Ventura county line. "Glorious clothes," says Lieberman.

Liberman keeps erratic hours of business because "maintaining our stock of special and unique items requires that we have flexible hours. We must travel far and wide to find them. When we are between appointments, please look for our sign, 'Open, please knock,' on the door. Browsers are welcome, but we ask that bridal customers schedule an appointment," says Lieberman.

Garments from this shop were seen in *Legends of the Fall, Titanic, The Legend of Bagger Vance, A Little Princess,* and *The Patriot.*

PLAYCLOTHES

$$

11422 Moorpark St., Los Angeles 91602; (818) 755-9559.
Open Mon–Sat: 11 a.m.–6 p.m., Sun: noon–5 p.m.

Owner: Wanda Solieau
Returns Policy: All sales final
Try-on Facilities: Dressing rooms with mirrors

Playclothes (one of Eden's favorite vintage stores) is a large airy space, full of color and sunlight and stocked with vintage clothing and accessories, including shoes, hats, and jewelry. This store is a terrific resource for middle priced vintage. Items are always in perfect condition and are organized into decades with color-coded tags. What's more, the sales staff (including Soileau) is knowledgeable about different eras and their styles. Eden's favorite find here was a pale green bias cut '30s evening gown and matching cape that she used on an actress portraying the Duchess of Windsor.

Owner Wanda Soileau counts Kim Bassinger, Molly Ringwald, Mark Harmon, Leah Thompson, and Bob Dylan as some of her celebrity clients. Soileau's customers span are all types and ages, but she reminds us that what is popular often changes. For now, she can't keep enough gowns in stock for all the women going to Hollywood events. Swing clothes from the '40s and early '50s are also hot, along with men's two-tone shoes and '50s wedge sandals.

You've seen their Western shirts in *Runaway Bride*, their womenswear in *Blast From the Past*, and '40s clothes in Woody Allen's *Company Man*. Costume designers from television's *The Drew Carey Show* and *Dharma & Greg* frequently shop here.

Soileau started collecting in Ohio in 1984 while still a professional dancer. Finding that vintage was not selling well in the Midwest at that time, she and her future husband moved to Los Angeles to start wholesaling their collection. Initially she sold at the Pasadena Rose Bowl swap meet and then out of their home. In 1995 Soileal opened a store in Studio City, and later moved to their current location in Toluca Lake.

Soileau and her musician husband travel extensively collecting vintage. Soileau can date almost any piece by design, color, hem length, fabric, and trim; she sometimes learns the exact history of the garment from the seller. Useful for both Hollywood costume designers and regular clients, Soileau will make shirts, pants, and jackets to order using vintage fabrics and patterns. This especially comes in handy for large or unusual sizes or for films where multiples are needed for the star and stunt double.

Diane Keaton wore a black vintage suit found in an LA vintage shop to the 1995 Oscars.

SIDE TRIP: San Diego

Anatomic Rag: 979 Garnet Ave., San Diego 92109; (858) 274-3597.

Boomerang's: 1435 University Ave., San Diego 92103; (619) 294-9669.

Buff: 1061 Garnet Ave., San Diego 92103; (858) 581-2833.

Buffalo Exchange: 3862 Fifth Ave., San Diego 92103; (619) 298-4411; or 1007 Garnet Ave., San Diego 92109; (858) 273-6227.

Flashbacks Recycled Fashions: 3847 Fifth Ave., San Diego 92103; (619) 291-4200.

Indigo Way: 437 Market St., San Diego 92101; (619) 338-0173.

Johnson House: 2706 Calhoun St., San Diego 92110; (619) 291-5170.

Life's Little Pleasures: 4219 Park Blvd., San Diego 92103; (619) 296-6222.

Memories Boutique: 1916 Cable St., San Diego 92107; (619) 224-8828.

Old Custom Inc. Denim Outlet: 8268 Miramar Rd., San Diego 92126; (858) 566-0212.

Rags The Fashion Exchange: 3940 Fourth Ave., San Diego 92103; (619) 229-1350.

Retro: 4879 Newport Ave., San Diego 92107; (619) 222-0220.

Shake Rag-Gaslamp: 432 F St., San Diego 92101; (619) 237-4955.

Tata Lane: 525 Evans Pl., San Diego 92103; (619) 688-9778.

Wear It Again Sam: 3823 Fifth Ave., San Diego 92103; (619) 299-0185.

What Ever: 6495 El Cajon Blvd., San Diego 92115; (619) 582-2006.

Cream of the Crop: 4683 Cass St., San Diego 92109; (858) 272-6601.

Crème de la Crème Resale Boutique: 10330 Friars Rd., San Diego 92120; (619) 282-5778.

Dress To Impress: 4242 Camino Del Rio North #9, San Diego 92108; (619) 528-9797.

Gentlemen's Resale Clothiers: 4695 Date Ave., La Mesa 91941; (619) 466-4560.

Great Curves: 2810 Lytton St., San Diego 92110; (619) 224-9174.

My Magnin: 10615 Tierrasanta Blvd. #A, San Diego 92124; (858) 268-2298.

Retro: 4879 Newport Ave., San Diego 92103; (619) 222-0220.

POLKA DOTS & MOONBEAMS

$$

8367 W. Third St., Los Angeles 90048; (323) 651-1746.
Open Mon–Sat: 11 a.m.–6:30 p.m., Sun: noon–5 p.m.

Owner: Wendy Freedman Borsck
Return policy: Next day exchange with receipt
Try-on Facilities: Two dressing rooms with large mirrors and flattering lighting

Polka Dots & Moonbeams offers vintage from the 1940s–70s with some turn-of-the-century pieces. The most interesting piece Borsck has collected is a Pucci jumpsuit. Her favorite period is the '40s because "the fabrics were of really good quality and they fit shapely women." A haunt of TV costume designers, clothing from this boutique has been seen on *Friends* and *Ally McBeal.*

REEL CLOTHES

$$

5525 Cahuenga Blvd., Los Angeles 91601; (818) 508-7762.
Open Mon–Sat: 10 a.m.–6 p.m., Sun: noon–5 p.m.
www.ReelClothes.com

Owner: Holly Haber, Elaine Vollmer, and Lennard Billin
Return policy: All sales final
Try-on Facilities: Three private dressing rooms with mirrors

Reel Clothes was established in 1981. "You've read the book. You've seen the movies. Now wear the clothes," said Vollmer, owner of "the world's first retail store specializing in the sale of wardrobe from movies and television." In 1991, Elaine's daughter Holly Haber was brought on board.

Haber, Vollmer, and Billin (mother, daughter, and husband/son-in-law) offer a piece of "Old Hollywood." At any given time, Reel Clothes has literally thousands of items for sale since newly consigned items arrive on a daily basis. Everything in their inventory was used in the production of a movie or television series, and everything comes directly from the studios or production companies. Clothing was usually worn or used by an actor or actress for just a few hours while filming a scene or two, is therefore still in perfect condition, and available at a fraction of the retail price. Just a few of the many films and TV shows include *The Cable Guy, Air Force One, As Good as It Gets, What Dreams May Come, Men in Black, Seven Years in Tibet,* and *Seinfeld.*

Here you might find a garment worn by Lisa Kudrow, Roseanne, Brad Pitt, Heather Locklear, Richard Gere, David Duchovny, Antonio Banderas, John Travolta, or Jennifer Love Hewitt. Apparel runs the gamut from designer fashion to casualwear. Armani, Boss, Varneyu's, and Lacroix are just some of the designer labels presented.

"Customers are often surprised to find more than one identical wardrobe piece," says Haber. Using the movie *Wild Things* as an example, she explains the need for multiples of the same outfit. "Shot in 100 degree heat and 80 percent humidity, the actors needed to change clothes during long days of shooting. While a character may have worn the same clothes every day—such as the blue tank top, black jean cutoffs, and sneakers worn virtually throughout the entire film—the actress, Neve Campbell, doesn't. So there were at least four different sets of Neve Campbell's outfit. That way the costumer could give her a clean set each time she reported to the set or if she wanted to change into clean clothes for her own comfort.

"The scene on the boat (at the end of the film) with Kevin Bacon and Matt Dillon required six days to shoot. Kevin Bacon wore at least six different versions of the same shirt with the marlin pattern."

RE-MIX

$$

7605 1/2 Beverly Blvd., Los Angeles 90036; (323) 936-6210.
Open Mon–Sat: noon–7 p.m., Sun: noon–6 p.m.
www.ReMixVintageShoes.com

Owner: Phil Health
Return Policy: Exchange only
Try-on Facilities: One dressing room

Re-Mix, a gallery-like space with rough walls and folk art furniture by Jon Bok, is the place to find never worn vintage and vintage reproduction shoes. "We love the idea that these shoes have been waiting for decades to reach their intended purpose—to be worn!" says Health. He scours warehouses, old stores, and manufacturers to keep this boutique filled with goodies. The most interesting pair collected in his travels? "A ladies redwing casual shoe from the '30s that looked like something Amelia Earhart would have worn. It is a brown, stacked two-inch pump with a kiltie and buckle straps, never worn, in a very wearable size 8 1/2." His favorite decades are the 1930s–50s, "because it was a very innovative period when MODERN was NEW; new materials were combined with traditional ones in never before seen styles with great quality and attention to detail."

RESURRECTION

$$$

8006 Melrose Ave., Los Angeles 90046; (323) 651-5516.
Open Mon–Sat: 11 a.m.–7 p.m., Sun: noon–5 p.m.

Manager: Tsoler Toumayan
Return Policy: All sales final
Try-on Facilities: Two dressing rooms with mirrors

Resurrection is the West Coast sister to the Resurrection in New York (see p. 202). This upscale, "simple but wild and rockin' store" at the toney west end of Melrose Avenue boasts a terrific collection of 1960s–80s leather jackets—from plain to highly decorative, including the "East Meets West" leather line from the '70s. This store also sells designer vintage from the '60s ("because it was such an experimental period"), '70s, and '80s for both men and women and includes Pucci, Gucci, Halston, North Beach, Courrèges, Eastwest Leather, Diane von Furstenberg and Emilio Pucci dresses, and Yves Saint Laurent '70s suits for men. Vintage denim is also plentiful.

Sales people are particularly friendly, but the merchandise is definitely aimed at customers with deep pockets. Specializing in the "avant-garde '60s, rockin' '70s, and fun '80s with a swipe of chic, this boutique offers the cream of the crop of LA vintage clothing. Clothing for rock 'n' rollers, unique party hosts and hostesses, and outerwear for the California breeze," says Toumayan. He personally collects Vivienne Westwood/Malcom McLaren punk clothing.

See this store's clothing in the film *Charlie's Angels*, a Jennifer Lopez video, and TV's *Ally McBeal, That '70s Show, Dharma & Greg,* and *Sex and the City.*

"Buying vintage is like being your own designer: You get to create a self-determined identity through clothes."
—LYNN HIRSCHBERG, "THE NEW OLD THING," *HARPER'S BAZAAR*, SEPTEMBER 2000

SHABON

$$

7617 W. Beverly Blvd., Los Angeles 90036; (323) 692-0061.
Open Mon/Tues and Thurs–Sat: noon–8 p.m., Sun: noon–6 p.m.

Owner: Rie Fujii
Return Policy: All sales final
Try-on Facilities: Dressing room with mirror

Shabon is Momo's (see p. 56) sister store. Specializing in '80s vintage (20 percent of which is new or remade) they stock Pucci, Gucci, Courrèges, North Beach Leather, and personal collections from independent designers in Japan and Paris. Shabon offers vintage that looks new and new clothes that look vintage. It all depends on what's currently in fashion, as "Shabon is more trendy than most vintage stores," says Fujii. Shabon also produces unique designs for this shop using vintage fabrics. They specialize in smaller sizes, sunglasses from all periods, vintage watches, belts, and hats.

A very stylish woman, Fujii hunts for boutique stock everywhere she travels (namely California, Paris, and Japan) to acquire the most cutting-edge merchandise. Shabon also offers a "wish list" for customers in search of something specific. Displayed in the shop entrance are current Japanese fashion magazines (*Cutie, EGG, Hawaii Girls, Crea, Viva*) along with pop and fashion books. "Positive" music is always played and an upbeat, knowledgeable staff available.

Fujii's personal collection includes three velvet Pucci suits (orange and pink, blue and lavender, brown and tan) and a North Beach Leather long jacket with scalloped bottom, so tiny "it fits and looks almost like a dress." Current offerings include: 1960s–80s vintage designer monogram bags from Gucci, LV, Pierre Jardin, Christian Dior, Coach, Bally, Courrèges, and Roberta (two Roberta velvet purses in perfect condition); amazing '70s beat-up tooled leather belts with big brass buckles; '80s thick belts in a variety of colors and buckles; and '60s sunglasses, including a huge brown Pierre Cardin pair and a clear Lucite dead stock pair with flowers made in France.

Snap Vintage Clothing

$

3211 Pico Blvd., Santa Monica 90405; (310) 453-4177.
Open Daily: noon–6 p.m.
www.SnapVintage.com

> **Owner:** David Meno
> **Return Policy:** Exchange or store credit within three days
> **Try-on Facilities:** Four dressing rooms with mirrors

Snap Vintage Clothing, located on the Westside of Los Angeles, is an unpretentious, postmodern industrial store, specializing in purses mainly from the '50s forward. What makes this store unique is its large collection of vintage purses eye-catchingly displayed five high on the west wall of the store in every size, shape, color, and style—lots of shiny materials and bright colors from the '50s and '60s. "My 22-year-old daughter suggested we carry handbags," says Meno. "No problems about sizing like with dresses or shoes. Most stores stock a few, but I decided a large selection would be much more enticing and a more exciting presentation. The most interesting are '50s poodle purses, of which we've had a few. Each one was unique in its own way and exciting for me to own, if only for a few days or weeks."

Snap also carries lots of cute rockabilly-type stuff that caters to a younger crowd. Merchandise is well-organized and hung with enough space between each item for easy viewing. Other popular items include '70s gear for customers looking for something to wear to theme parties. Meno's favorite decade is the '50s—a whimsical and daring time of using colors like pink and black together. "The quality of the fabrics was also exceptional. Just as the cars were wild and bold, so were the clothes—great decade for fashion exploration of style, design, and color."

TV's *Felicity*, *Buffy the Vampire Slayer*, and *Providence* have shown their wares.

CHLOË SEVIGNY wore a white 1969 (Holly) Harp gown to the 2002 *Vanity Fair* Oscar party.

STAR SHOES: A COCKTAIL LOUNGE AND VINTAGE SHOE SALON

$$

6364 Hollywood Blvd., Los Angeles 90028; (323) 462-STAR (7827).
Open Thurs–Sat: 6 p.m.–11 p.m.

Owner: John Nixon and Paul Devitt
Return Policy: All sales final
Try-on Facilities: Not needed, shoes only

Star Shoes is truly a unique store. Where else but in Hollywood can you enjoy an evening of cocktails and the latest music while trying on fabulous vintage shoes? Only at Star Shoes, the brainchild of owner Nixon. His dream was to open a theme bar, and when he became aware of the availability of the Joseph LaRose collection of shoes and handbags from the '40s to the '70s, there was his answer! La Rose was a prominent "cobbler to the stars" in a past Hollywood era whose influence can still be seen in the current designs of Gucci and Jimmy Choo.

Nixon was born and raised in Los Angeles and has always been fascinated by the past, whether architecture, art, cars, or music. But he also likes to look forward, and hopes his club will be a platform to showcase innovative ideas from designers, photographers, and artists of all types. Located in an old building near the famed Hollywood and Vine intersection, shoes are displayed in beautiful glass cases, with the bar and dance floor toward the back. Framed vintage shoe ads decorate the dark paneled walls. Open since September 2001, Star Shoes has succeeded all expectations. However, no fear of running out of vintage shoes; the collection has over 120,000 pairs—plus handbags.

Additional Vintage Stores

Buffalo Exchange: 131 N. La Brea Ave., Los Angeles 90036; (323) 938-8604.

Denim Doctors, Inc.: 8044 W. Third St., Los Angeles 90048; (323) 852-0171.

Junk for Joy: 3314 W. Magnolia Blvd., Burbank 91505; (818) 569-4903.

Rebecca's Dream: 16 S. Fair Oaks Ave., Pasadena 91105; (626) 796-1200.

Repeat Performance: 318 N. La Brea Ave., Los Angeles 90036; (323) 938-0609.

Retro Clothing: 6439 Hollywood Blvd., Los Angeles 90028; (323) 466-8863.

RockaHula: 7560 Melrose Ave., Los Angeles 90046; (323) 653-1951.

Second Debut: 3309 W. Magnolia Blvd., Burbank 91505; (818) 848-8800.

Yellowstone Clothing, Inc.: 712 N. La Brea Ave., Los Angeles 90038; (323) 931-6616.

DESIGNER RESALE

THE ADDRESS BOUTIQUE

$$$

1116 Wilshire Blvd., Santa Monica 90401; (310) 394-1406.
Open Mon–Sat: 10 a.m.–6 p.m., Sun: noon–5 p.m.
www.TheAddressBoutique.com

> *Owner:* Maureen Clavin
> *Return policy:* All sales final
> *Try-on Facilities:* Open dressing room with lots of mirrors

The AdDress Boutique, a modern, skylit store, carries everything from casualwear to glamorous ball gowns with an emphasis on dressy clothes. This store has it all, including Chanel, Valentino, Bob Mackie, Fabrice, Sonia Rykiel, DKNY, St. John, Escada, Balenciaga, Adolfo, Bill Blass, Prada, Missoni, Jil Sander, Versace, Lagerfeld, Richard Tyler, Oscar de la Renta, and Dolce & Gabbana. Handbags and shoes are top of the line, from designers like Manolo Blahnik, Chanel, and Gucci.

Elizabeth Kaye chronicled the history of Clavin's store in "Salvation Armani" for *Los Angeles Magazine* in January 2001. In 1963, Clavin was watching the women at the Hillcrrest Country Club parading their magnif-icent Oleg Cassini and Rudi Gernreich gowns when she had the idea to open her own resale store. These women, she realized, wouldn't dare be seen in the same gown twice, which meant that every one of them must have clos-ets filled with designer clothes that they were never again be able to wear. Clavin borrowed a small comercial space in Manchester from a dentist friend and began collecting cast-offs from her friends. Stylish garments flooded in; she tagged the garments at greatly reduced prices, split the pro-ceeds with the former owners, and, despite the stigma of wearing "used" clothing at that time, founded a successful and viable business.

Clavin opened the AdDress Boutique in 1986 after establishing her repu-tation as a fashion-savvy retailer and hiring an equally stylish and dedicated staff. Over the years, she has gained access to the closets of many celebrities, buying clothes for her store from stars like Natalie Wood, Zsa Zsa Gabor, and Joan Collins.

People used to only whisper that they had been to a resale store. Today, pro-fessional women from all over the world shop resale. Current offerings include: a Pamela Dennis sequined and embroidered hip-length jacket in shades from taupe to gray, accented with pink flowers; a black Chanel V-neck dress with a front slit and low fishtail back in a striped pattern; a black *peau de soie* Valentino couture gown with ostrich feathers on bust worn by a famous celebrity (who is also a customer); a beautiful lime chiffon Dior worn on the runway of the Paris spring 2000 show; and a deeply discounted, brand-new Oscar de la Renta beaded gown, complete with the original price tag.

Clavin's personal collection includes the dress that Zsa Zsa Gabor was arrested in, the dress that Joan Collins wore when she was introduced to the Queen of England, and Madonna's touring jacket from her *I Can Dance* album.

"Mostly I just look for a really cool garment—something that worked back then and is still great now."
—MARK BRIDGES, COSTUME DESIGNER FOR *BLOW* AND *SIX FEET UNDER*

CASUAL COUTURE, INC.

$$

13900 Ventura Blvd., Los Angeles 91423; (818) 990-4743 or (877) 990-1193.
Open Mon–Sat: 9:30 a.m.–6 p.m.
www.CasualCouture.com

> *Managers:* Eugene Winnik and Vanessa Young
> *Return policy:* Exchange or store credit only
> *Try-on Facilities:* Four large fitting rooms with mirrors

Casual Couture, Inc. is a 2,500-square-foot, clean, organized store with Greek décor. Garments, found in excellent condition, are arranged by color not size. This boutique carries top designer fashions from all over the world. Look for Alaïa, Thierry Mugler, Moschino, Missoni, Valentino, Emanuel Ungaro, Richard Tyler, Christian Lacroix, Dolce & Gabanna, Versace, Gucci, Prada, Escada, Donna Karan, Chanel, St. John, and Calvin Klein. Black-tie, business attire, sporty, funky, selective vintage, brand new to pre-worn, in petite to larger sizes…there's something for everyone.

CLOTHES HEAVEN

$$$

110 E. Union St., Pasadena 91103; (626) 440-0929.
Open Tues–Sat: 11ish a.m.–5ish p.m.
www.ClothesHeaven.com

> *Owner:* Larayne L. Brannan
> *Return policy:* All sales final
> *Try-on Facilities:* Dressing room with mirror

Clothes Heaven offers a fabulous selection to choose from; updated suits, casualwear, eveningwear, shoes, and accessories—all in superb or gently worn condition. Many of the pieces are consigned from couture representatives, some have been used in studio wardrobes, and others come from celebrity closets, stylists, CEOs of corporations, fashion designers, and models. "We receive items from closets in such diverse areas as Malibu, Beverly Hills, Santa Barbara, La Jolla, New York, Arizona, and Texas," says Brannan.

Looking for the perfect shoe? Current stock includes: Chanel black satin three-inch pumps with gold insoles and a thin band detail on the toe; Prada red loafers to wear with tweeds and flannels; and sexy Chanel sling-back sandals highlighted with gold chain detail and three-inch heels.

Currently showing: a Prada creamy vanilla velvet slip dress with dainty beaded straps, a beaded empire waist, and beautiful black jet beads embellishing the front and back; a Thierry Mugler shapely deep sage suit fashioned from wool waffle weave, featuring the signature Mugler hourglass waist and fully lined and accented with whimsical silver shooting stars at the snap closures; and a hand-rolled silk 34-inch Chanel scarf, stitched in a wine color with emerald and gold adornments.

CROSSROADS TRADING COMPANY

$$

7409 Melrose Ave., Los Angeles 90046; (323) 782-8100.
Open Mon–Sat: noon–8 p.m., Sun: noon–7 p.m.
www.CrossRoadsTrading.com

Owner: Varies
Return Policy: Store credit within seven days with tag attached and receipt
Try-on Facilities: Spacious dressing rooms with mirrors and locking doors

Crossroads Trading Company locations include San Francisco, Sacramento, Oakland, San Jose, Seattle, Berkeley, Stockton, Santa Cruz, and Los Angeles. They take great pride in having "the best selection of merchandise for their customers and specialize in the most current labels and styles." They do not buy clothing for resale that has holes, stains, or rips. Their company motto is "look good, feel good," and they are confident that their customers do both. Clean, bright, and well-organized, the store is colorful with an urban industrial theme. Their range of labels and designers include Gap, Banana Republic, J.Crew, Abercrombie & Fitch, BCBG, bebe, Bisou Bisou, Diesel, Club Monaco, Levi's, Big Star, Express, Calvin Klein, DKNY, Marc Jacobs, Prada, Manolo Blahnik, Betsey Johnson, Helmut Lang, and Gucci.

DECADES TWO LLC
$$$

8214 Melrose Ave., Los Angeles 90046; (323) 655-1960.
Open Mon–Sat: 11:30 a.m.–6 p.m. or by appointment.
www.DecadesTwo.com

> *Owner:* Christos Carrinos and Cameron Silver
> *Return policy:* All sales final
> *Try-on Facilities:* Large, private dressing room, with three-way mirror

Decades Two LLC, the "Barney's" of designer resale, features merchandise from celebrities, stylists, and fashion editors as well as samples direct from designers. They carry the best of current high-end designer clothing such as Prada, Chloé, Helmut Lang, and Chanel for discriminating customers who want high style for low prices, according to Carrinos and Silver. Source of merchandise? The best dressed folks from all over the world.

Decades Two takes credit for starting the Alaïa trend. At one time they had hundreds of pieces. "Azzedine Alaïa does not think of himself as a fashion designer. Rather, he likes to call himself a *bârisseur*—a builder or a couturier-architect. His designs emphasize structure and purity of form. The fabrics and rigorous tailoring are constructed to envelop the body snugly; each garment is hand-finished."

The signature Alaïa look began to emerge in the early '80s with riveted leather, industrial-zipped dresses, a predominance of knit fabrics, and experimental mixes of lace and leather, silk jersey and tweed. In 1994, he showed long dresses in "houpette," a stretchy, new fabric that molds to the body. The following year he made clothes out of "Relax," an anti-stress fabric with carbon-dipped fibers that repel electromagnetic waves. NASA used it for wall and floor coverings. His hemlines are impervious to the dictates of fashion. They can run from upper-thigh to ankle-length within the same collection.

What is constant, however, are tailoring and cut that follow the same principles as corset making—the use of stays, whalebones, lace-ups, and décolletage to flatter the figure and highlight the bust. Alaïa disappeared from the scene in the mid-'90s but made a major comeback in spring 2000, when his structured silhouettes suddenly became the hippest thing around—again.

Located in an art deco building with 14-foot ceilings, Decades Two currently stocks a plethora of classic leather quilted Chanel handbags; a Marc Jacobs cotton dress with rhinestone pearl attachments; and samples from Ungaro, Tracey Reese, and Plenty.

GREAT LABELS

$$$

1126 Wilshire Blvd., Santa Monica 90401; (310) 451-2277.
Open Mon–Fri: 11 a.m.–7 p.m., Sat: 10 a.m.–6 p.m., Sun: noon–5 p.m.

      Owner: Andrea Waters
  Return Policy: Case by case basis
Try-on Facilities: Four large dressing rooms with full-length mirrors

Great Labels is an 1,800-square-foot elegant boutique that carries hip contemporary designers like Vivienne Tam, Vertigo, Trina Turk, Theory, Richard Tyler, Prada, and Miu Miu. "My personal background involved working for Calvin Klein and Donna Karan on a national level," says Waters, "but my love for clothes and shopping introduced me to resale." For the past five years Waters learned the business and is now the proud owner of her own boutique that specializes in gently used contemporary clothing, shoes, handbags, and accessories.

Waters' most fabulous find, now in her personal collection, is a Prada gown worn to the Academy Awards.

LISA'S NY STYLE RESALE

$$$

13531 Ventura Blvd., Los Angeles 91423; (818) 788-2142.
Open Mon–Sat: 11 a.m.–6 p.m. or by appointment.

Owner: Lisa Beth Zohar
Return Policy: All sales final
Try-on Facilities: Private fitting rooms

Lisa's NY Style Resale is bright, relaxed, and eclectic; the walls are covered with interesting outfits, scarves, jewelry, and hats, including some ethnic pieces such as Chinese robes. An ex-New Yorker, Lisa Zohar's store reflects the colorful and artistic personality of its owner. Zohar says she is not at all label-conscious; she looks for pieces that are original, different, and fun to wear.

There are plenty of serious pantsuits and businesswear, and currently a bright red Geoffrey Beene sheared mink coat trimmed with ostrich feathers is also for sale. At the other end of the spectrum, the $10 room has finds such as a white silk pantsuit by INC. Zohar will stay open by appointment if needed to accommodate the working woman's busy schedule and will do personalized searches for customers who are looking for something specific.

"I carry every designer—from couture high-end to wonderful boutique clothing—including Armani, Chanel, St. John, Yves Saint Laurent, Richard Tyler, and Moschino, and an extensive collection of vintage jewelry. I love unusual and different pieces in everything from today's fashions to vintage pieces from the '30s to '80s," says Zohar. "Glamorous clothing is wonderful, and I love unusual fabrics, patterns, and styles. I like to pick the pieces of an era with glitz, sophistication, and intrigue."

TV's *Felicity* and *Dharma & Greg* have wardrobe from this boutique.

P.J. LONDON

$$$$

11661 San Vicente Blvd., Los Angeles 90049; (310) 826-4649.
Open Mon–Sat: 10:30 a.m.–6 p.m., Sun: noon–5 p.m.
www.PJLondon.com

Owner: Phyllis Davis
Return policy: Next day exchange
Try-on Facilities: Five private dressing rooms with mirrors

P.J. London is where to find the latest fashions at a fraction of the retail cost. This upscale consignment shop features a collection of high-quality, pre-worn clothing that is current and impeccably cared for. Davis has been in business for over 15 years, offering the finest designer clothing and accessories by Chanel Boutique, Ralph Lauren Collection, DKNY, St. John, Jean Paul Gaultier Femme, Calvin Klein, Cartier, Armani, Dries Van Noten, Plantation, Thierry Mugler, Hervé Léger, Dolce & Gabbana, Issey Miyake, Todd Oldham, TSE, Richard Tyler, Vivienne Westwood, Alaïa, People of the Labrynths, Gigli, Gucci, Jil Sander, Moschino, Matsuda and Yamamoto.

"I carry real jewelry and fake and old costume jewelry. I love '40s costume jewelry such as Miriam Haskell. We have shoes galore that range from Manolo Blahniks to Miu Miu to Prada to Weitzman. We have Fendi bags that have never been used. We have Chanel and Bottega bags as well. The fun part is never knowing what will arrive in the store each and every day," says Davis. This is one of a handful of resale stores that also carries wedding gowns.

Lots of celebrities and society people consign here, though Davis carefully guards her client list. Current treasures: a Claire collection long, beaded gown in blue; a Maxfield Parrish leather jacket; Fendi shoes with matching wallet; a new Fendi bag with encrusted jewels; and 15 pairs of Manolo Blahniks— many never used.

THE PLACE & CO.

$$$

8820 S. Sepulveda Blvd., Los Angeles 90045; (310) 645-1539.
Open Mon–Sat: 10 a.m.–6 p.m.
www.ThePlaceandCo.com

Owner: Joyce Brock
Return policy: All sales final
Try-on Facilities: Large private dressing rooms with mirrors

The Place & Co. is the place for resale designer clothing, where fashions of the stars become the affordable attire of savvy and stylish women and men who visit from around the world. Clothes worn by the likes of Elizabeth Taylor, Bette Midler, Dyan Cannon, Anjelica Houston, Tori and Candy Spelling, Joan and Jackie Collins, and Jay Leno are sold with the proceeds going to their favorite charity.

"We were the first designer resale store in the country, after Encore in New York," says Brock. In business for 37 years, this 4,000-square-foot store is separated into three areas—career sportswear, eveningwear, and forward fashion sportswear; you will also find accessories. Everything is top quality, including Armani, Gucci, Prada, Escada, St. John, Richard Tyler, Thierry Mugler, Badgley Mischka, Bill Blass, and Sonia Rykiel—all 65 to 85 percent off retail prices. There is also a large collection of Judith Leiber beaded handbags—particular favorites of Brock's. Current finds include: a black Chanel dress and stole, embroidered with the Chanel logo; 50 pairs of Chanel shoes, all new; and a Gianfranco Ferré three-piece outfit of beaded chiffon in bronze and blue.

"Look at everything. When you think you have finished, go back and look again."
—RUTH MYERS, OSCAR-NOMINATED COSTUME DESIGNER FOR *EMMA*

77

RAVISHING RESALE

$$$

8127 W. Third St., Los Angeles 90048; (323) 655-8480.
Open Tues–Sat: 11:30 a.m.–6 p.m. or by appointment.

Owner: Maruschka
Return policy: All sales final
Try-on Facilities: Three dressing rooms and several full-length mirrors

Ravishing Resale, a peach and green store, plays classical music to accompany contemporary Armani, Chanel, Escada, Hermès, Richard Tyler, Pamela Dennis, Dolce & Gabbana, and Moschino, all sold alongside vintage pieces.

A recent visit turned up a fabulous '50s white Saga mink stole with removable white mink tassels (previously owned by Phyllis Diller) in immaculate condition and a '70s elegant Jean Louis hand-painted silk organza gown with fishtail hem worn by Loretta Young. And how about this showstopper? A Karl Lagerfeld (circa 1989) cream silk sparkle gown, halter-style, that looks like a Marilyn Monroe dress, and is full length and adorned with celestial glitter and crystals.

Maruschka specializes in high quality and designer contemporary clothes because "my customers like wearing expensive clothes at unbelievable prices. I am extremely selective about clothes I accept on consignment, and they all are in excellent condition—some with tags still attached. In fact when people come in at first glance they think they're in a fashionable boutique and not a resale store."

"I used a wonderful red 1930s blouse on Kate Hudson in *Almost Famous*, as my research told me that it was in the '70s that we really started getting into vintage. It was a romantic period, post-hippy, pre-glam. We had no money, and leather and lace just seemed to come together."

—BETSY HEIMANN, COSTUME DESIGNER FOR *ALMOST FAMOUS* AND *VANILLA SKY*

REPLAY

$$$

147 S. Los Robles Ave., Pasadena 91101; (626) 793-3987.
Open Tues–Sat: 10:30 a.m.–5:30 p.m.

> ***Owner:*** Betty Stein
> ***Return policy:*** All sales final
> ***Try-on Facilities:*** Three large fitting rooms with full-length mirrors

Replay is a New York-style boutique with a lovely garden entry. Gathered from over 3,500 individual consignors, as well as store overruns, Stein specializes in current chic clothing for the working professional with St. John Knits, DKNY, Anne Klein II, Calvin Klein, Dana Buchman, David Hayes, Ellen Tracy, Platinum, Jones New York, and Armani and offers new arrivals daily in size 2 to 26.

Stock currently includes: a lovely light blue St. John knit suit with sparkle trim from their spring 2002/Cruise collection; a zip-front jacket dress in black knit (silk and spandex) by Wayne Rogers; and new seconds from Johnny Was/J. Jill at "giveaway prices."

"Some years ago Replay received hundreds of new items when an Amen Wardy store closed. A customer purchased a particularly lovely gown from this group and wore it to a ball where [fashion critic] Mr. Blackwell commented on its beauty," says Stein. Interested in a never-worn gown from the Amen Wardy store (with the original price tag of $12,000 still on it)?

Replay has been across the street from the Hilton Hotel since Stein opened it in 1981. "On several occasions visiting divas staying at the Hilton Hotel across the street found better gowns to wear that very evening for their local performance," says Stein. "Another time a regular customer received a last minute invitation to attend the Academy Awards. Lucky for her she remembered a fabulous gown she had seen at Replay. Not only did she get a knockout dress but at a bargain price!"

Replay II, owned by Stein's daughter, is just down the street at
105 S. Los Robles Ave., (626) 793-4501.

RITZ RESALE

$$$

50 N. Mentor Ave., Pasadena 91106; (626) 449-3528.
Open Tues–Sat: noon–6 p.m.
www.RitzResale.com

       Owner: Liz McDuffie
    Return Policy: All sales final
Try-on Facilities: Large dressing room

Ritz Resale has specialized in the sale of new and pre-owned women's clothing and accessories since 1979. Current styles of designer and brand names, such as TSE, Philippe Adec, Escada, Prada, and Mui Mui, are displayed in a comfortable setting with wood beams and a cement floor.

Currently in stock: new Prada mules in black leather; an Escada two-piece sweater set in periwinkle rayon and viscose; and a like-new Chanel black, wool crêpe pantsuit. One of McDuffie's most fabulous finds was a Russian sable coat, consigned by KCET public television station, appraised at $80,000 by Saks Beverly Hills and sold for $6,600. An Angela Bassett fan? McDuffie sells clothes from all of her films, including a fringed leather jacket that she wore and wardrobe from *How Stella Got Her Groove Back.* "We also consign a lot of high-end, 'after sale' items from boutiques," adds McDuffie.

SILENT PARTNERS

$$

99 E. Union St., Pasadena 91103; (626) 793-6877.
Open Tues–Sat: 11 a.m.–5 p.m.

       Owner: Alyce Doney
    Return policy: Case by case basis
Try-on Facilities: Two areas with mirrors

Silent Partners is housed in a charming one-room, freestanding building. Doney carries great outfits from defunct TV sitcoms, including *Who's the Boss* and *Designing Women*. She also carries all the jewelry from Universal Studios' wardrobe department along with garments by Anne Klein, Issey Miyake, Ferragamo, Ellen Tracy, Escada, Sonya Rykiel, and Chanel. "Our original premise was to have a shop infused with the top popular designers with clothes for every occasion," she says.

The most interesting piece she has collected is from Marion Marshall Wagner (Robert's second wife), who gave Doney a blouse made of antique lace in black and red, which she still treasures. Current offerings include Hermès leather-trimmed grey wool pants and several Gucci wool skirts and jackets trimmed in leather. If you're in the market for glamour, ask about their Jean Louis pieces.

Additional Resale Stores

Armani Wells: 12404 Ventura Blvd., Los Angeles 91604; (818) 985-5899.

Laura's Designer Resale Boutique: 12426 Ventura Blvd., Los Angeles 91604; (818) 752-2835.

Lily et Cie: 9044 Burton Way, Beverly Hills 90211; (310) 724-5757.

Second Debut: 3309 W. Magnolia Blvd., Burbank 91505; (818) 848-8800.

San Francisco

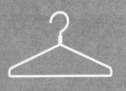

AAARDVARK'S ODD ARK

$

1501 Haight St., San Francisco 94117; (415) 621-3141.
Open Sun–Thurs: noon–8 p.m., Fri/Sat: 11 a.m.–9 p.m.

Owner: Joe Stromei
Return Policy: All sales final
Try-on Facilities: Dressing rooms with outside mirrors

For more details, see **Aaardvark's Odd Ark** Los Angeles on p. 46.

AMERICAN RAG COMPAGNIE

$$

1305 Van Ness Ave., San Francisco 94109; (415) 474-5214.
Open Mon–Sat: 10 a.m.–9 p.m., Sun: noon–7 p.m.
www.AmRag.com

Owner: Mark and Margot Werts
Return Policy: All sales final
Try-on Facilities: One dressing room with mirror

For more details, see **American Rag Compagnie** Los Angeles on p. 47

OLD VOGUE

$$

1412 Grant Ave., San Francisco 94133; (415) 392-1522.
Open Sun–Tues: 11 a.m.–6 p.m., Wed: 11 a.m.–8 p.m., Thurs–Sat: 11 a.m.–10 p.m.

Owner: Dan and Michelle Nuelle
Return Policy: Exchange/store credit within one week
Try-on Facilities: Three dressing rooms with mirrors

Old Vogue, a clean, straightforward shop with more "substance than style," specializes in men's vintage clothing. They carry 1950s–60s hats, suits, shirts, cashmere overcoats, topcoats, pants, and sweaters, all hand-picked by owner Dan Nuelle. Looking for clean, crisp, perfectly faded 501 Levi's? This shop has over 400 pairs in every size imaginable. Old Vogue also carries a limited stock of women's vintage. Says Nuelle, "We specialize in this merchandise because it's what we can find, and it sells because it's clothing that people can actually wear every day."

Customers run the gamut. "Our first famous shopper (16 years ago) was Leonard Bernstein. He bought a vintage letter sweater and had no qualms about asking for a discount! We only recognized him when he gave us his American Express card, just like in the commercials. He was really sweet! Lauren Hutton (about 13 years ago) bought five vintage Hawaiian shirts. Our employee was so starstruck she undercharged her by $150! Ricky Lee Jones and Rita Coolidge first met at our store. Rita Coolidge was playing at the Fairmont Hotel at the time.

"Tom Waits buys hats from us, and Hal Ketchum bought a really cool sharkskin suit from us about six years ago. Rob Schneider has been shopping at our store since the very beginning, even before he became famous. And Danielle Steele came in about 12 years ago when her girls were still babies. It was the entire entourage including the nanny. She bought quite a few things, including a vintage railroad conductor's hat. We also get a lot of musicians who come in and buy stage clothes, but to tell you the truth we hardly recognize anyone."

"As for accessories, I tend to use vintage jewelry, because I can almost guarantee that you won't see anyone else wearing the same thing. I just buy what I love, and I've been collecting for years."

—JANE JANIGER COSTUME DESIGNER FOR *PASSIONS*

RETROFIT VINTAGE

$$

910 Valencia St., San Francisco 94110; (415) 550-1530.
Open Sun/Mon and Wed: noon–7 p.m., Tues: 1:30 p.m.–7 p.m.,
Thurs: 1:30 p.m.–8 p.m., Fri/Sat: noon–8 p.m.

Owner: Alison Doekstra and Audrey Wackerly
Return Policy: All sales final
Try-on Facilities: Submarine door opens to vaulted dressing room
with scattered mirrors

Retrofit Vintage carries Gucci, Courrèges, Saks, Chanel, North Beach Leather, Climax, and Lilli Ann. The sometimes kitschy, sometimes classic rotating front window display is a reflection of the store's focus on vintage sportswear. They specialize in clothes "that are comfortable to run around the city in. We mix eras and styles, vintage and contemporary. We also have fun and fancy dresses for parties and events, lots of jackets, leather, fake fur, and denim." Owners Hoekstra and Wackerly's favorite era is the '60s because it represents a period where fashion met rock 'n' roll in a very "sexy way; frivolous and flattering with lots of attitude."

Current offerings include: 1960s–80s men's and women's leather jackets; vintage purses and bags, from clutches to airline workout bags; and 1960s–80s dresses.

THIRD HAND STORE

$$

1839 Divisadero St., San Francisco 94115; (415) 567-7332.
Open Mon–Sat: noon–6 p.m.

Owner: Joseph A. Dowler
Return Policy: Exchange or store credit only
Try-on Facilities: Dressing room and mirrors

Third Hand Store has specialized in the 1890s–1940s since their opening in 1967, although owner Dowler's favorite period is the '20s, because he "enjoys the androgynous and creative aspects of this time."

Current offerings include: a '20s raccoon opera coat; a black silk and lace empire dress with jet beading; and a Scottish paisley cape with green silk brocade lining and monkey fur trim.

Additional Vintage Stores

Arc of San Francisco: 2101 Mission St., San Francisco 94110; (415) 626-5710.

Argentina Gift Shop: 3250 24th St., San Francisco 94110; (415) 824-3488.

Clothes Contact: 473 Valencia St., San Francisco 94103; (415) 621-3212.

Departures from the Past: 2028 Fillmore St., San Francisco 94115; (415) 885-3377.

Fashion Exchange: 1215 Polk St., San Francisco 94109; (415) 441-1331.

First Chop: 954 Irving St., San Francisco 94122; (414) 564-7030.

Getups: 4028 24th St., San Francisco 94114; (415) 643-8877.

Good Byes: 3483 Sacramento St., San Francisco 94118; (415) 674-0151.

Guys & Dolls Vintage: 3789 24th St., San Francisco 94114; (415) 285-7174.

Held Over: 1543 Haight St., San Francisco 94117; (415) 864-0818.

La Rosa Vintage: 1711 Haight St., San Francisco 94117; (415) 668-3744.

Mr. Toad's: 1015 Quesada Ave., San Francisco 94124; (415) 822-8789.

Nu2u2: 2415 Mission St., San Francisco 94110; (415) 550-0115.

Regina Co.: 5845 Geary Blvd., San Francisco 94121; (415) 386-8577.

Retro City Fashions: 1543 Haight St., San Francisco 94117; (415) 621-3520.

Satellite Vintage: 1364 Haight St., San Francisco 94117; (415) 626-1364.

Schauplatz Clothing & Furniture: 791 Valencia St., San Francisco 94110; (415) 864-5665.

Seconds To Go: 2252 Fillmore St., San Francisco 94115; (415) 563-7806.

Suit Yourself Boutique: 101 Spear St. #A21a, San Francisco 94105; (415) 777-5181.

Ver Unica: 148 Noe St., San Francisco 94114; (415) 431-0688.

Vickie's Street Shop Boutique: 603 Haight St., San Francisco 94117; (415) 552-5997.

Vintage Sport Limited: 780 Joost Ave., San Francisco 94127; (415) 587-5827.

"I've found that vintage clothing, especially from the '30s to the '60s, was made to be very body conscious. Back then, they used curved seams so even inexpensive garments seemed to be better made and more flattering."
—MARY E. VOGT, COSTUME DESIGNER FOR *MEN IN BLACK*

DESIGNER RESALE

CROSSROADS TRADING COMPANY
$$

1901 Fillmore St., San Francisco 94115; (415) 775-8885.
Open Mon–Thurs: 11 a.m.–7 p.m., Fri/Sat: 11 a.m.–8 p.m.,
Sun: noon–6 p.m.
www.CrossRoadsTrading.com

Owner: Varies
Return Policy: Store credit within seven days with tag and receipt
Try-on Facilities: Spacious dressing rooms with mirrors and locking doors

For more details, see Crossroads Trading Company Los Angeles on p.72.

Also at 1519 Haight St., San Francisco 94117; (415) 355-0555.

JANE CONSIGNMENT "A BREATH OF FRESH WEAR"

$$

2249 Clement St., San Francisco 94121; (415) 751-5511.
Open Tues–Sat: noon–8 p.m.

> **Owner:** Jane Willson
> **Return Policy:** All sales final
> **Try-on Facilities:** Three dressing rooms with mirrors

Jane Consignment (formerly Heather's Boutique) is a fun, colorful shop with buttercream walls and purple trim; it has a "homey feel," like being in a friend's living room. Offering designers like Chanel, St. John, Versace, Donna Karan, Ferragamo, and Bruno Magli, Willson's goal is to have something for everyone who walks in her store. She hopes to make it a fun experience, from picking out an outfit to completing it with shoes and jewelry. "I enjoy consigning unusual pieces," says Willson, "such as Egyptian scarves, vintage purses, and crystal from the '40s, and an antique silk burgundy kimono with cream trim." These rarities are found among a selection of contemporary designer resale.

Willson's favorite period is the '40s, for not only the fashion, but also for its music and values. "It was a time of great pride in the country's war effort, and woman definitely dressed in keeping with their new found entry into the work-place, as well as with sensuality in their day-to-day lives."

Current offerings include: a St. John's classic navy knit suit with signature buttons; beautiful Chanel beige knit sleeveless dress in two layers with jacket/cape accented with signature buttons; and Versace black satin jeans with signature buttons and patch.

KIMBERLEY'S CONSIGNMENTS

$$–$$$

3020 Clement St., San Francisco 94121; (415) 752-2223.
Open Tues–Sat: 11 a.m.–5 p.m., first Sun of the month: 11 a.m.–3 p.m.
www.kimberleys.com

Owner: Toni Petersen
Return Policy: All sales final
Try-on Facilities: Two dressing rooms with three-way mirrors

Kimberley's Consignments is a plain, simple store where the merchandise speaks for itself. Labels include Chanel, Escada, Jil Sander, Dolce & Gabbana, and Ellen Tracy and are rounded up from individual consignors from all over the country. Petersen has been with this store since her teens—it passed from the previous owner to her mother, then to her—and she knows the business from the inside out. This store has evolved from selling anything and everything in past years to today's stock of fine quality clothing. "We now attract wonderful clients with wonderful clothing," says Petersen. "Whole families now consign with us, some for the past 30 years. We have a very special relationship with our clients, which is one of the reasons I love this business."

High-end merchandise might include an 80-carat sapphire necklace. More down-to-earth offerings include: a rack of current Chanel eveningwear in fine, beautiful fabrics; a large selection of Hermès scarves and ties; an all-weather mink-lined Hermès coat; and 18K bumble bee pins with ruby eyes from the '50s.

Peterson's favorite period is…everything—except the '60s and '80s. Because she personally sews, she can't help but be impressed with the designs of the '30s and '40s, but since "I specialize in current trends, that is my priority."

DEMI MOORE wore a no-label vintage lavender gown from the '40s to the 1992 Oscars.

REPEAT PERFORMANCE
$$

2436 Fillmore St., San Francisco 94115; (415) 563-3123.
Open Mon–Sat: 10 a.m.–5:30 p.m.
www.sfsymphony.org

Owner:	San Francisco Symphony, Jeannette Garbarini-Walters, Retail Manager
Return Policy:	Case by case basis
Try-on Facilities:	Two dressing rooms with full-length mirrors and good lighting

Repeat Performance, San Francisco Symphony's resale shop, has been located on Fillmore Street for over 30 years. All profit goes to support the symphony. Since merchandise is obtained from symphony patrons, symphony leagues, and local Pacific Heights neighborhood donors, this store maintains a high standard of what they will accept and has a good reputation for quality, stylish goods at low prices. Items not accepted for resale are passed along to Goodwill.

"We are known as being the top resale shop in the neighborhood and have a loyal following. Our motto is 'You never know what you will find,' as we change our stock daily," says Garbarini-Walters. This store offers a couture sale once a year of top "runway" designer goods, such as Galliano, Commes de Garçons, and Yves Saint Laurent. Current offerings include St. John Knits, Armani, DKNY, Chanel, and Hermès.

WORN OUT WEST
$$

582 Castro St., San Francisco 94114; (415) 431-6020.
Open Sat–Thurs: noon–7 p.m., Fri: noon–8 p.m.

Owner:	Wray-Martin Corp
Return Policy:	All sales final
Try-on Facilities:	Dressing rooms with mirrors

Worn Out West specializes in resale men's clothing and includes "biker" leather (chaps, jackets, pants), Western wear, and military uniforms—think along the lines of Village People fashion.

Additional Resale Stores

Ceces Closet: 1781 Church St., San Francisco 94131; (415) 695-0578.

Consignment Boutique at Next: 2226 Fillmore St., San Francisco 94115; (415) 440-1500.

Cris: 2056 Polk St., San Francisco 94109; (415) 474-1191.

Designer Consigner: 3501 Sacramento St., San Francisco; (415) 440-8653.

Geary Consignment Boutique: 6300 Geary Blvd., San Francisco 94121; (415) 831-8565.

Heather's Boutique: 2249 Clement St., San Francisco 94121; (415) 751-5511.

Mary's Exchange: 1302 Castro St., San Francisco 94114; (415) 282-6955.

Mi Mum's Treasures: 2105 Van Ness Ave., San Francisco 94109; (415) 440-7299

Wasteland: 1660 Haight St., San Francisco 94117; (415) 863-3150.

Way to Array: 431 Stockton St., San Francisco 94108; (415) 743-9999.

Denim fabric has been used for hundreds of years, with its origins in 16th or 17th century Europe. Yet in its modern incarnation as blue jeans, it has remained one of the most contemporary and cutting edge fabrics.

1853: Leob Strauss starts a wholesale business, supplying gold miners with strong, durable clothes. His use of copper rivets to attach the pockets boosted his workpants to the top of the market.

1930s: Hollywood popularizes the Western, complete with blue jean-wearing cowboys. Jeans begin to loose the status of workwear and become associated with American individualism.

1940s: Fewer jeans are made during WW II, but American soldiers sometimes wear them off duty, introducing them to the world. After the war, Wrangler and Lee begin to compete with Levi's for a share of the new, burgeoning market.

1950s: *Rebel Without a Cause* and James Dean, the icon of the teenage rebel, popularize denim with young people. Jeans are banned at some schools across the United States as they become a symbol of defiance against authority.

1960s–70s: Decorated denim appears, supplementing the fashions of the '60s: embroidered jeans, painted jeans, and psychedelic jeans, catering to a marketplace of hippies and flower children. The Smithsonian adds jeans to it's American History collection, while in many non-western countries, jeans are a symbol of Western decadence, and though highly coveted, are difficult to obtain.

1980s: Designers begin putting their names on jeans, elevating them to high-fashion status.

SEATTLE

FRITZI RITZ CLASSIC CLOTHING

$$

3425 Fremont Pl. North, Seattle 98103; (206) 633-0929.
Open Tues–Fri: noon–6 p.m., Sat: noon–5:30 p.m., Sun: noon–5 p.m.

Owner: Sylvan Johnson
Return Policy: Case by case basis
Try-on Facilities: Two large dressing rooms with '40s tailor's full-length mirrors

Fritzi Ritz Classic Clothing has been in Seattle for the past 28 years. Along with carrying accessories Johnson loves, such as bags, shoes, and hats, this store will also clean and block your vintage hats. Johnson offers an excellent stock of accessories from the '40s and '50s, as well as a selection of purses from the '60s. Selected offerings of retro looks from the present are also available, because "they fit everybody!" An example of their stock might be a '40s shoulder-strap green crocodile bag with matching black suede and green gauntlet croc gloves. Johnson's favorite period is the '40s, because the clothes were "romantic and work for day or eveningwear."

ISADORA'S

$$$

1915 First Ave., Seattle 98101; (206) 441-7711.
Open Mon–Thurs: 11 a.m.–6 p.m., Fri: 11 a.m.–8 p.m.,
Sat: 10 a.m.–6 p.m., Sun: noon-5 p.m.
www.Isadoras.com

Owner: Laura Dalesandro
Return Policy: Exchange or store credit only
Try-on Facilities: Private dressing rooms with mirrors

Isadora's, located in downtown Seattle one block from the famous Pike's

Place Market, carries men and women's clothing, jewelry, and accessories. They also carry collectible costume, antique, and fine estate jewelry (jewelry valued over $1,000 comes with an appraisal by a certified gemologist) and a full line of formalwear for men. Isadora's sister Internet company, Valentinasgifts.com, carries lovely antique clothing and jewelry.

Isadora's garments are in excellent condition. Several years ago owner Laura Dalesandro, who has been buying and selling fine vintage clothing for over 28 years, started her own line of exquisite wedding dresses reminiscent of the '20s and '30s. Although you'll find garments from many different eras, they specialize in the years 1900–70 and offer only the best in design and quality of any particular decade. They try to have as many designer pieces as possible, including vintage Adrian, Lilli Ann, Eisenberg, and Dior suits dating from 1900–60, all garments of great design and wonderful fabrics. "Beaded suits are our favorite," says Dalesandro.

Current stock includes: a fabulous black evening suit with beaded jacket: a '50s vintage grey mink stole with a raised collar; and a beautiful '70s evening dress in gray blue silk jersey by designer Dominic Rompollo.

LE FROCK
$$

317 E. Pine St., Seattle 98122; (206) 623-5339.
Open Mon–Sat: 10 a.m.–7 p.m., Sun: noon–5 p.m.
www.LeFrockOnline.com

Owner: Diane Stone
Return Policy: All sales final
Try-on Facilities: Two dressing rooms upstairs

Le Frock carries an eclectic mix of pure vintage with interesting contemporary clothing and accessories for men and women. Enter this shop through towering black and white curtains to shop for Armani, Versace, Hugo Boss, Dolce & Gabanna, and Prada while listening to the melodic sounds of Billie Holiday. "Personally," says Stone, "we love pre-'50s, '30s bias cut dresses, and '40s men's and women's gabardine suits." Fabulous finds include: a white lace Thierry Mugler suit in mint condition; silk velvet capes; and men's and women's hats.

Le Frock has been at this location for the last ten years. They even have an adorable "Bargain Loft" of specially priced belts, bags, and clothes for men and women.

....

THE OLA WYOLA BOUTIQUE
$

2211 First Ave., Seattle 98121; (206) 448-3325.
Open Mon–Wed: noon–6 p.m., Thurs/Fri: 2 p.m.–6 p.m., Sat: noon–5 p.m.
www.belltunes.com

> **Owner:** Renee Bonow-Marnier and Elaine Bonow
> **Return Policy:** Exchange or store credit only
> **Try-on Facilities:** Dressing room and mirrors

The Ola Wyola Boutique is an eclectic store in trendy Belltown, located down one flight of stairs in a basement next to a ballet studio. This well-organized shop offers clothing, shoes, and accessories in two large rooms. Business hours can be erratic, and there is no elevator. They carry dancewear plus great, handpicked items of funky vintage clothes, silk nightgowns from Asia, shoes, and accessories. "We like the '50s and '60s," says Bonow, "but we do get cool stuff from the '70s and '80s."

"I have a great fondness for old clothes. They were not expensive then, and they are not expensive now. The new versions at the mall are twice the price of the originals."

—JANE RUHM, FOUR-TIME EMMY NOMINEE,
COSTUME DESIGNER FOR *TRACEY TAKES ON*

OLD DUFFERS STUFF

$$

1519 First Ave., Seattle 98101; (206) 621-1141.
Open Tues–Sun: noon–5 p.m.

Owner: Karen D. Swanson
Return Policy: All sales final
Try-on Facilities: One small fitting room

Old Duffers Stuff specializes in classic, timeless fashion. "Quality that doesn't exist in this day and age. I recycle the best of the past in men's and women's fashions," says Swanson. This shop is only 700 square feet, but you will find a good designer mix such as Eisenberg & Sons, Paul Sachs, Leslie Fay, Dior, Vera Wang, and Chanel. Swanson's favorite eras are the '50s and early '60s because "everything was fitted to compliment every figure." She also likes '30s bias cut dresses, slips, and teddies, "vintage clothes that are union made, no sweatshops, no pollution." Current stock includes a '40s fur jacket with a Chevron design and 975 white and brown ermine tips.

PRIVATE SCREENING

$$

1530 Melrose Ave., Seattle 98122; (206) 839-0759.
Open Mon–Sat: 11 a.m.–6 p.m., Sun: 11 a.m.–5 p.m.

Owner: Gary Mortenson
Return Policy: All sales final
Try-on Facilities: Two dressing rooms

Private Screenings are two eclectic stores that specialize in the classic styles of the 1920s–50s—"eras of the true designers, clothing made to fit the body," says Mortenson. "Plus rockabilly and Western." Gathered from estate sales and private collections, they offer '20s prints, fabrics, and lots of lingerie for women, and '40s fedoras and tailored suits for men. Mortenson's private collection includes a two-tone "Ricky" jacket, complete with daggers and fleur-de-lis.

Also at 3504 Fremont Pl. North, Seattle 98103; (206) 548-0751.

Additional Vintage Stores

Atlas Clothing Co.: 1515 Broadway, Seattle 98122; (206) 323-0960.

Fury: 2810 E. Madison St., Seattle 98112; (206) 329-6829.

Red Light: 312 Broadway East, Seattle 98102; (206) 329-2200; and 4560 University Way Northeast, Seattle 98105; (206) 545-4044.

Yesterdaze: 1501 Pike Pl. #315, Seattle 98101; (206) 521-0572.

DESIGNER RESALE

ALEXANDRA'S
$$$

412 Olive Way, Seattle 98101; (206) 623-1214.
Open Mon–Thurs and Sat: 10 a.m.–6 p.m., Fri: 10 a.m.–7 p.m.

Owner: Alexandra Oncken
Return Policy: All sales final
Try-on Facilities: Private dressing rooms with mirrors

Alexandra's is a retail-style boutique located downtown in a historical Times Square building behind Westlake Center. This upscale boutique offers current designer clothing and accessories by Armani, Chanel, Escada, Donna Karan, Prada, St. John, Richard Tyler, Faconnable, Ralph Lauren, Max Mara, DKNY, Dolce & Gabbana, Moschino, Catherine Regehr, TSE, Valentino, Calvin Klein, Ellen Tracy, Sonia Rykiel, Loro Piana, and Versace gathered from high-fashion consigners.

"In the ten years we've been in business, our customers have come to expect a savings of 70 to 90 percent off original prices, and we offer the largest selection of designer clothing and accessories in the Northwest. Our current designer labels are in near-new condition, plus new boutique, end-of-season items. Our stock ranges from professional daywear to a large selection of evening and cocktail, designer casualwear, coats, skiwear, and resort in sizes 2 through 18, plus a huge line of accessories," says Oncken.

CROSSROADS TRADING COMPANY

$$

325 Broadway East, Seattle 98102; (206) 328-5867.
Open Mon–Sat: 11 a.m.–7 p.m., Sun: noon–7 p.m.
www.CrossRoadsTrading.com

> *Owner:* Varies
> *Return Policy:* Store credit within seven days with tag attached and receipt
> *Try-on Facilities:* Spacious dressing rooms with mirrors and locking doors

For more details, see **Crossroads Trading Company**, Los Angeles on p. 72.

GYPSY TRADER

$$$

3517 Stone Way North, Seattle 98103; (206) 547-1430.
Open Tues–Sat: 10 a.m.–6 p.m., Sun: noon–5 p.m.
www.GypsyTrader.com

> *Owner:* Paula O. Baker and Gregory S. Baker
> *Return Policy:* All sales final
> *Try-on Facilities:* Four dressing rooms with mirrors

Gypsy Trader is an eclectic, diverse store that offers contemporary and ethnic clothing with some vintage. The Bakers stock business and casual in sizes ranging from 4 to 26; all are carefully selected, one-of-a-kind clothing treasures. "I also have mud cloth from West Africa, alpaca sweaters, scarves and shawls from Peru, silk scarves from India, and a wonderful selection of jewelry from all over the world along with some great vintage pieces," says Baker.

The owners' pet dog and store mascot, Mishka, a longhaired German shepherd, not only works alongside the owners but hosts her very own page on their web site.

This store's merchandise is very much in keeping with its owner's motto: "Life is a never-ending treasure hunt."

VENUS
$$

1015 E. Pike St., Seattle 98122; (206) 322-5539.
Open Tues–Sat: noon–9 p.m.
www.VenusClothes.com

Owner: Julia Kaplan
Return Policy: All sales final on consigned goods
Try-on Facilities: Three big dressing rooms with sturdy benches

Venus sells to large, spicy, and empowered Goddesses (size 14 and up) and specializes in hard to find items such as corsets, leather, PVC, and gothic in good quality. "Our consignment strives to be quality and unusual," says Kaplan, who carries Tonya Winters, Stormy Leather, Goddess Venus, and their own gothic line, Myth Demeanors.

"Personally, I love the English Edwardian period [1905–early 1920s]," says Kaplan. "Not too frilly, very severe, kind of like the '40s in America. It appeals to the headmistress in me! Overall, I think 'funky and elegant' describes my store and me. I try to fit large women and make them feel sexy!

"We have created a warm, comfortable, and lush atmosphere to mirror the voluptuousness of Venus, the goddess of love, art, and beauty. We are committed to beauty and ease for larger women. We start at size 14 and go up as high as we possibly can. Our clothes are reasonably priced and run the gamut of styles. We carry everything, including work clothes, play clothes, formal gowns, gothic, dresses, leather, shoes and boots, jewelry, and accessories." To make your shopping experience more comfortable, Kaplan offers magazines and plus-size catalogs to browse through, couches, spacious dressing rooms, and lots of chocolate!

Additional Resale Stores

Hello Gorgeous: 411 E. Pine St., Seattle 98122; (206) 621-0702.

VANCOUVER

BLUE UNICORN SHOP

$$–$$$

3136 Oak St., Vancouver V6H 2L1; (604) 734-5924.
Open Tues–Thurs: 11 a.m.–6 p.m., Fri: 11 a.m.–7 p.m., Sat: noon–6 p.m.

Owner: Patty Jackson
Return Policy: All sales final
Try-on Facilities: Dressing room and mirrors

Blue Unicorn Shop owner Patty Jackson has been in business for 22 years at the same location, carrying vintage from the 1930s–60s, contemporary resale clothing, and vintage-inspired pieces. She also rents clothes for parties and films and recently sold some gorgeous 1950s and 1960s watches to a property master from Lions Gate Studio.

This store is eclectic and fun, decorated with photos from the '40s and '50s, and home to lots and lots of costume jewelry, vintage shoes, men's fedoras, the occasional '80s leather jacket, Capri pants, and an immaculate 1940s leather suitcase. Jackson tells us that "Hillary Swank was a recent customer, looking for beaded cardigans."

Born on the East Coast, Jackson says she grew up at a time when her stylish mother still had 1950s clothes in her closet. "This is part of me, I will always do this."

BURCU'S ANGELS FUNKY CLOTHING

$

2535 Main St., Vancouver V5T 3E5; (604) 874-9773.
Open Tues–Sat: 11 a.m.–8 p.m., Sun/Mon: noon–6 p.m.

Owner: Burcu Ozdemir
Return Policy: Gladly accepted
Try-on Facilities: Dressing room and mirrors

Burcu's Angels Funky Clothing does not sell clothes—Ozdemir sells "color, texture, fun, and magic." Merchandise, organized by color rather than size or period, is mostly from the 1970s, but the '30s and '40s are also well-represented.

Born and raised in Turkey, Ozdemir says she comes from a background of bartering and trading, which she encourages in her store. A box outside the store is available 24 hours a day for people to take or leave donations. How does she make a profit? She believes in the "gypsy tradition—if you don't have to spend money, you probably will." Ozdemir also encourages returns. "I'd rather that people give back what they don't like and get something they do," she says.

Her clients range from "young folks—teenagers are introduced to the free box and the concept of exchange—to the older folk from the bingo parlor down the street who like bright colors to musicians and a number of cross-dressers," says Ozdemir.

DELUXE JUNK COMPANY

$$

310 Cordova St. West, Vancouver V6B 1E8; (604) 685-4871.
Open Mon–Sat: 10 a.m.–6 p.m., Sun: noon–6 p.m.
www.DeluxeJunk.com

Owner: Ken Spada
Return Policy: Exchanges on first-priced items within four days
Try-on Facilities: Dressing rooms and mirrors

Deluxe Junk Company's Ken Spada has been in this location since 1984 and in business since 1973. Spada says the store is "as funky as you can get but very clean." Every garment is cleaned, repaired, and steamed before being put out for sale, and no clothing is hung on harmful wire hangers. He carries vintage ("the older the better, because I just like it") from Victorian forward, plus some contemporary fashion, all of which is on consignment. To keep the merchandise fresh and always moving, the price goes down 25 percent after 30 days and an additional 50 percent a month later.

The film industry in Vancouver does a lot of its shopping at Deluxe Junk, since "we have 100 years of clothing here." A Jack the Ripper film, an Arnold Schwarzenegger film, and TV shows such as *Smallville* have used dozens of Victorian pieces. "Money is secondary," says Spada. "I just love clothes!" Costume jewelry, especially rhinestone pieces from the '40s and '50s, is plentiful.

LEGENDS RETRO-FASHION
$–$$

4366 Main St., Vancouver V5V 3P9; (604) 875-0621.
Open Wed–Sat: 11 a.m.–5:30 p.m., Sun: noon–5 p.m.

Owner: Diane LeBlanc
Return Policy: All sales final on vintage
Try-on Facilities: Two dressing rooms

Legends Retro-Fashion owner LeBlanc started in the '60s as a Seattle "flower child" frequenting thrift shops, and her business just emerged as a "hobby gone right." Her store, at its present location for 12 years, is small but attractive. She features styles from the '50s and '60s but will carry anything from the turn of the century forward. LeBlanc is known for her sequined and beaded sweaters and blouses, plus her costume jewelry and rhinestones. Her clientele ranges from teens to collectors to costume designers for films. Author Eden purchased some jewelry and hats here while in Vancouver designing a Tony Danza pilot.

Additional Vintage Stores

Cabbages & Kinx: 315 Hastings St. West, Vancouver V6B 1H6; (604) 669-4238.

"Fashions fade, style is eternal."
—YVES SAINT LAURENT

ACT II BOUTIQUE

$$$

2599 16th Ave. West, Vancouver V6K 3B9; (604) 733-5515.
Open Tues: 10:30 a.m.–5 p.m.

Owner: Mary McDougall
Return Policy: All sales final
Try-on Facilities: Three dressing rooms

Act II Boutique has been in business for 18 years and carries high-end labels such as Armani, Max Mara, Escada, and St. John Knits. There is also a selection of shoes, purses, scarves, and accessories. At the end of the season there is a giant sale, and anything left over is donated to shelters for battered women.

TURNABOUT COLLECTIONS LTD.

$$–$$$

3121 Granville St., Vancouver V6H 3K1; (604) 732-8115.
Open Mon–Sat: 10 a.m.–6 p.m., Sun: noon–5 p.m.
www.turnaboutclothing.com

Owner: Joy Mauro (Lapka)
Return Policy: All sales final
Try-on Facilities: Dressing room and mirror

Turnabout Collections Ltd. has two locations: Granville Street carries business and eveningwear for women, while West Broadway, billed as "a store full of threads for the relaxed West Coast lifestyle," offers casual clothing and popular labels for women and men.

Mauro, a Vancouverite with a passion for fashion, opened Turnabout on South Granville in 1978 when she was 23 years old. "We were the first consignment shop in Vancouver to be more than just a yard sale or bazaar," said Mauro. "We opened a fresh, modern retail store." Mauro's insatiable appetite for fashion, sense of adventure, and youthful enthusiasm proved contagious.

"I love clothes and I love the concept of having something different to wear all the time. There's the thrill of surprises, the rush of the new outfit," she says. "Whoever says you can't buy happiness doesn't know where to shop!" Turnabout offers, among other popular designers, Chanel, Armani, Prada, Versace, Gap, and Calvin Klein.

"We're known for professional, efficient, and honest service." After more than 20 successful years of consigning experience in prime neighborhoods, Turnabout boasts a list of 5,000 consignors. "We pride ourselves in providing flavorful, colorful, varied merchandise. Our consigners shop the world. We're all things to all people, from the everyday working girl to Hollywood movie glitz and glitter."

Also at 3060 W. Broadway, Vancouver V6H 1E3; (604) 731-7762.

....

WEAR IT AGAIN SAM
$$

1070 W. Broadway, Vancouver V6H 1E2; (604) 739-9327.
Open Mon–Fri: 10:30 a.m.–6 p.m., Sat 11 a.m.–5 p.m.

Owner: Morganne Dancer
Return Policy: All sales final
Try-on Facilities: Three dressing rooms

Wear It Again Sam reflects the owner's personal taste with its feminine, romantic décor: cozy armchairs, flowers, and candy bowls on the tables. Merchandise ranges from casual to businesswear, with some eveningwear. "Vancouver women don't dress formally for evening much," says Dancer, "but I love to dress up and I tell them to dress glamorously just for themselves."

She currently carries a brand-new Armani leather three-quarter coat for an unbelievably low price because, as luck would have it, the Armani rep from Italy stopped by her store and, rather than take the sample back to Italy, sold it to Dancer. Mr. Jax, a Vancouver designer of some popularity, is also available here.

Additional Resale Stores

Bon Retour: 1097 Broadway West, Vancouver V6H 1E2; (604) 739-3434.

Changes Consignment Clothing: 4330 Tenth Ave. West, Vancouver V6R 2H7; (604) 222-1505.

Dragon & Phoenix: 6248 East Blvd., Vancouver V6M 3V7; (604) 261-1317.

14 Plus Consignment: 3636 Fourth Ave. West, Vancouver V6R 1P1; (604) 731-9975.

Front Consignment Clothing: 3746 Main St., Vancouver V5V 3N7; (604) 879-8431.

Happy Three Clothing Co Ltd.: 2824 Granville St., Vancouver V6H 3J5; (604) 733-2982.

Happy Three II New & Consignment: 3629 Fourth Ave. West, Vancouver V6R 1P2; (604) 730-9638.

In-Again Clothing: 1962 Fourth Ave. West, Vancouver V6J 1M5; (604) 738-2782.

Kisa's of Kerrisdale Consignment: 2352 41st Ave. West, Vancouver V6M 2A4; (604) 266-2885.

N20: 2009 41st Ave. West, Vancouver V6M 1Y7; (604) 266-8411.

SALT LAKE CITY

THE BAG LADY BOUTIQUE
$–$$

241 E. Broadway, Salt Lake City 84111; (801) 521-6650.
Open Mon–Sat: 11 a.m.–6 p.m.

Owner: Melissa Baber
Return Policy: All sales final
Try-on Facilities: Three dressing rooms with mirrors

The Bag Lady Boutique carries vintage and contemporary designer resale pieces; labels range from the '50s designs of Suzy Perette to the contemporary clothing of BCBG, bebe, Ann Taylor, J.Crew, and Banana Republic. "I specialize in what is currently in retail stores," says Baber, "but also enjoy offering whatever is unique and well made, has stood the test of time, and items that simply evoke an emotional response." Baber's most interesting offering? "Without a doubt, the dress collection of a certain Chanel model— dresses from the model's teen years in the 1950s. Beautifully made garments with exquisite detailing."

Current stock includes: a '40s-style, cream silk dress in a green whimsical pattern; men's short-sleeved Western-style shirts, and a Ms. Pioneer vintage, fitted denim jacket with stitched detail and leather piping. Baber's favorite period is the '50s, "mainly for the colors and fabrics. I have a weakness for '50s house wares and furniture."

nastassja kinski wore a coordinated vintage 19th-century necklace, earrings, and dinner ring set of gold, diamonds, and semi-precious light-green peridots, to the 2000 Oscars.

"It seems that styles come and go very fast, and some people's bodies just aren't made to wear the current trend. Wear what looks good on you and not just the latest style."
—SCILLA HERNANDEZ, COSTUME DESIGNER FOR *DAWSON'S CREEK* AND *PARTY OF FIVE*

SIDE TRIP: DENVER

VINTAGE

Ace Dry Goods: 78 S. Broadway, Denver 80209; (303) 733-2237.

All American Vogue: 10 S. Broadway, Denver 80209; (303) 733-4140.

Flossy Mc Grew's: 1824 S. Broadway, Denver 80210; (303) 778-0853.

Irene's: 2342 S. Colorado Blvd., Denver 80222; (303) 759-3010.

DESIGNER RESALE

Anna's Near New Boutique: 1244 S. Sheridan Blvd., Denver 80232; (303) 934-3322.

Encore Shop: 125 Adams St., Denver 80206; (303) 321-1305.

Lisa Marie's: 4418 Tennyson St., Denver 80212; (303) 433-2344.

Mercer Place: 2371 E. Evans Ave., Denver 80210; (303) 765-4776.

Profile Upscale Resale: 7400 E. Hampden Ave. # 10, Denver 80231; (303) 779-4151.

Puttin on the Ritz: 1446 S. Colorado Blvd., Denver 80222; (303) 759-4398.

Repeat Boutique: 2725 S. Colorado Blvd., Denver 80222; (303) 757-0086; or 7495 E. Iliff Ave., Denver; (303) 755-9204.

Second-Hand Rose-Ann Clothing: 3426 E. 12th Ave., Denver 80206; (303) 321-5530.

Snob Shop: 2804 E. Sixth Ave., Denver 80206; (303) 355-6939.

Super Seconds: 130 W. 84th Ave., Denver 80260; (303) 427-9078.

Twice as Haute: 600 Downing St., Denver 80218; (303) 753-6003.

Wardrobe Works: 138 W. 12th Ave., Denver 80204; (303) 446-8446.

GRUNTS & POSTURES

$–$$

779 E. 300 South, Salt Lake City 84102; (801) 521-3202.
Open Mon–Sat: 10 a.m.–7:30 p.m., Sun: noon–6 p.m.

Owner: Timothy O'Brien
Return Policy: Store credit only
Try-on Facilities: Four dressing rooms with mirrors

Grunts & Postures offers mostly vintage pieces from the 1920s–70s, along with a few contemporary resale items such as Gap and J.Crew. Owner O'Brien's favorite eras are the '30s and '40s because of their simplicity of design and wonderful detailing, resulting in understated clothing that's equally flattering to men and women. Current offerings include '50s Western and Hawaiian shirts and lots of retro partywear, such as large collared shirts and bell-bottom jeans from the '70s.

DESIGNER RESALE

CASSANDRA'S CLOSET, INC.

$–$$

3355 S. Highland Dr., Salt Lake City 84106; (801) 484-2522.
Open Mon: noon–5 p.m., Tues–Fri: 11 a.m.–6 p.m., Sat: 11 a.m.–5 p.m.

Owner: Suzi Berrett
Return Policy: All sales final
Try-on Facilities: Five dressing rooms, two three-way mirrors in store

Cassandra's Closet offers a selection of beautiful furs, exquisite jewelry, and elegant beaded dresses among their designer and high-end items. Although predominately contemporary designer resale pieces are offered, vintage jewelry and accessories are also part of Berrett's stock. In business for 18 years, Berrett's goal is "to make nicer, more expensive things afford-able to everyone." Why? "Because that's what sells!" Current offerings include: a yellow two-piece St. John Knit pantsuit; an ivory Dana Buchman silk wrap dress; several Chanel purses, in black, red, and navy; and a Ferragamo purse and heels in pewter.

Additional Resale Stores

Consignment Circuit: 1464 E. 3300 South, Salt Lake City 84106; (801) 486-6960.

Fetish Designer Consignment: 790 E. 9400 South, Sandy 84094; (801) 816-0223.

Garp's Merchantile: 627 S. State St., Salt Lake City 84111; (801) 537-1357.

NameDroppers: 2350 E. 21st South, Salt Lake City 84111; (801) 474-1644.

Yours, Mine & Ours: 177 W. 300 South, Bountiful 84010; (801) 299-1515.

LaS vegas

THE ATTIC

$$

1018 S. Main St., Las Vegas 89101; (702) 388-4088.
Open Mon–Fri: 10 a.m.–6 p.m., Sun: 11 a.m.–6 p.m.
www.theatticlasvegas.com

Owner: Victor and Mayra Politis
Return Policy: All sales final
Try-on Facilities: Nine small, mirrored cubicles

The Attic stands out from the moment you see its purple, turquoise, zebra-striped exterior. Inside there is even more fun to be had.

There are two stories and 10,000 square feet in all. The upstairs ("The Attic") is all vintage. There is lots of merchandise to choose from, with the emphasis on funky rather than classic. Everything from vintage cowboy boots, '70s shirts, plaid polyester pants, fun-loving jackets, belts, jewelry—you name it, they have it.

The downstairs is full of remade vintage, designed by the talented owner Mayra Politis with the help of a seamstress "who understands the look." Politis says that whenever a vintage piece can be rescued, embellished, or combined with something else, a new piece of retro clothing is created. Currently in stock is a black vintage bra, covered with new pink silk roses; a lime green pair of polyester low-rise pants with a paisley appliqué rescued from an old muumuu; and a rack of miniskirts in everything from Chinese brocades to chevron (striped) wools. For the men who love partywear there are shiny disco shirts, Austin Powers ruffled shirts, and what Politis lovingly calls "Pimp Daddy" shirts. Men's 1970s platform shoes can also be made to order. At the higher end are custom fur coats, such as one made of faux cheetah, interspersed with stripes of netting, and lined with a bronze "mock crocodile" brocade.

Customers include Carrot Top, David Spade, Courtney Cox, local Las Vegas talent, and even (for a party) the Governor and First Lady of Nevada!

RETRO VINTAGE CLOTHING
$–$$

906 S. Valley View Blvd., Las Vegas 89107; (702) 877-8989.
Open Tues–Sat: noon–6 p.m.
www.ebaystores.com/retrovintageclothing

> ***Owner:*** Melina Crisostomo
> ***Return Policy:*** All sales final
> ***Try-on Facilities:*** Dressing room

Retro Vintage Clothing is located in a small mall in the Northwest area of Las Vegas. Crisostomo calls her store a "European-styled boutique," and it was nominated for Best Vintage Store in *Las Vegas Life* magazine.

She has a $5 rack outside and higher priced treasures inside, including lots of women's shoes, cotton summer dresses, and Hawaiian shirts for the men.

VALENTINO'S ZOOT SUIT CONNECTION
$$–$$$

906 S. Sixth St., Las Vegas 89101; (702) 388-4088.
Open Mon–Sat: 11 a.m.–5 p.m.

> ***Owner:*** Beverly and Valentino K. Parker
> ***Return Policy:*** All sales final
> ***Try-on Facilities:*** Two fitting rooms

Valentino's Zoot Suit Connection has been in the business of vintage fashion for over 25 years, first in Los Angeles and recently in Las Vegas. This store is a generous 17,000-square-feet, and is tightly packed with vintage apparel and some new lines with a retro look, such as Davinci shirts and Avanti silk Hawaiian shirts. "It is hard to find authentic vintage in larger men's sizes," says Valentino, hence the XXLs he carries.

Valentino loves '40s glamour, and his specialty is custom-made zoot suits, which come in 22 colors and start at around $800. Many of the local performers come to him for zoot suits and costumes of all kinds for their nightclub acts.

Additional Vintage Stores

Buffalo Exchange: 4110 S. Maryland Pkwy. #1, Las Vegas 89119; (702) 791-3960.

DESIGNER RESALE

FASHION EXCHANGE
$–$$

6985 W. Sahara Ave. Ste. 101, Las Vegas 89117; (702) 247-1230.
Open Mon–Fri: 10 a.m.–6 p.m., Sat: 10 a.m.–5 p.m.

Owner:	Linda J. Haney
Return Policy:	All sales final
Try-on Facilities:	Two mirrored dressing rooms and full-length wall mirror

Fashion Exchange's owner Haney carries all the major upscale labels as well as mid-range and younger labels such as DKNY and bebe, so that all ages can find something, whether it's for a barbecue or a black tie affair. "It's so exciting to help a client dress for a job interview or a mother find the right gown for her daughter's wedding, especially since they don't have to worry that someone else will have the same outfit," says Haney. She also carries beautiful wedding dresses and fur coats, which are available during the winter.

"A well-made garment," remarks Haney, "can be timeless. With a little imagination you can create the perfect outfit if you wear clothes that fit your body style." She likes to help clients dress a designer piece up or down with the perfect accessories and shoes. This store has an art deco look and a calm atmosphere. Haney's most interesting find was a white coat adorned with Mickey and Minnie Mouse from Euro Disney.

TAKE II BOUTIQUE

$–$$$

3400 S. Jones Blvd. #12, Las Vegas 89146; (702) 876-8480.
Open Mon–Sat: 10 a.m.–5 p.m.

Owner: Robin Reddle and Muriel Covington
Return Policy: All sales final
Try-on facilities: Five dressing rooms, three with three-way mirrors

Take II Boutique, at this location for 13 years, has a lovely Victorian garden theme, complete with plants and a fountain. High- to low-end designer labels are carried—everything from Chanel to Jones New York in sizes 2 to 22. They once found a beautiful collection of New York-designed vintage hats and purses and promptly offered these treasures in their store.

Reddle and Covington will ship purchases anywhere but most enjoy helping their in-store clients coordinate items so they leave the shop looking "boutiquely chic," says Reddle. Their favorite period of fashion is "NOW! Because the women of today want to look in style and put together."

Additional Resale Stores

Elite Repeat Boutique: 4439 W. Flamingo Rd., Las Vegas 89103; (702) 220-4499.

Ritzy Rags Designer Resale Boutique: 2550 S. Rainbow Blvd. # W3, Las Vegas 89146; (702) 257-2283.

A Second Chance: 2797 S. Maryland Pkwy. # 29, Las Vegas 89109; (702) 734-2545.

DALLAS

AHAB BOWEN

$$

2614 Boll St., Dallas 75204; (214) 720-1874.
Open Mon–Sat: noon–6 p.m., Sun: 1 p.m.–5 p.m.

Owner: Michael Longcrier
Return Policy: All sales final
Try-on Facilities: Two dressing rooms with mirrors

Ahab Bowen is housed in a restored Victorian house that dates from the late 1800s and specializes in clothes from the 1920s–70s for men and women. Offerings include pants, tops, skirts, dresses, coats, robes, and jackets from the 1940s–70s, and dresses, lingerie, coats, hats, and jewelry from the 1920s–30s. Longcrier stocks men's shirts, as well as a good selection of '40s rayon dresses. The current trend is toward more ethnic designs, such as sheer, embroidered '60s blouses.

Additional Vintage Stores

Fifth Avenue Rags: 17610 Midway Rd. #132, Dallas 75287; (972) 248-7337.

Gratitude: 3714 Fairmount St., Dallas 75219; (214) 522-2921.

Puttin' on the Ritz: 6615 Snider Plz. #201, Dallas 75205; (214) 369-4015.

Ragwear: 2000 Greenville Ave., Dallas 75206; (214) 827-4163.

S & P Trading Company: 6104 Luther Ln., Dallas 75225; (214) 369-8977.

 wore a 1963 vintage Lanvin Castillo gold gown to the 2002 Oscars.

ANONYMOUSLY YOURS

$–$$$

204 Abrams Forest Shopping Ctr., Dallas 75243; (214) 341-4618.
Open Mon–Fri: 10 a.m.–6 p.m., Sat: 10 a.m.–5:30 p.m.
www.AYResale.com

Owner: René Bankston
Return Policy: All sales final
Try-on Facilities: Five dressing rooms with mirrors

Anonymously Yours is over 1600 square feet of shopping, from business to bridal (400 bridal gowns are on display at all times), with labels from Liz Claiborne to Vera Wang. Gowns range from very formal to relaxed; designers include Alfred Angelo, Maggie Sottero, Jim Hjelm, and Mori Lee. Bankston offers alterations, pressing, and cleaning services for all of their bridal gowns. Current offerings include: a Chanel suit in green; a Vera Wang informal silk bridal gown; and an "excellent selection of blouses from Ann Taylor and Dana Buchman."

Bankston loves to mix and match clothes of many different periods to achieve new and different looks. Her most interesting collectable? A 1957 Cadillac that was featured in *High Life* magazine.

"There's a playfulness to certain periods that doesn't exist any more. There is also craftsmanship that doesn't exist any more...Vintage clothes are worn and weathered, but have withstood the passage of time."

—JEFFREY KURLAND, OSCAR-NOMINATED
COSTUME DESIGNER FOR *BULLETS OVER BROADWAY*

GENTLY OWNED
MEN'S CONSIGNERY

$$

17610 Midway Rd. #108, Dallas 75287; (972) 733-1115.
Open Mon–Fri: 11 a.m.–7 p.m., Sat: 11 a.m.–5 p.m.
www.GentlyOwned.com

Owner: Todd Shevlin
Return Policy: All sales final
Try-on Facilities: Private dressing rooms with mirrors

Gently Owned Men's Consignery has been in the Midway Road location for seven years, specializing in outfitting men from head to toe in contemporary designer resale. In his "little Neiman-Marcus" corner of the world, Shevlin offers suits, shirts, sports coats, vests, and shoes from designers like Armani, Canali, Ermenegildo Zegna, Hart Schaffner & Marx, Hickey-Freeman, Burberry, Tallia, Jhane Barnes, and Polo; everything from formalwear to business-casual to casual. "We match up our clients' personal sense of style to the best the world of fashion has to offer. Our clients are discriminating shoppers who seek great quality combined with great value.

"Imagine a business," adds Shevlin, "where you help people get their dreams. Add to that the satisfaction of seeing my customers realize their dreams by shopping with me. They love walking out of my store equipped with everything they're going to need to dress for success."

Also at 2926 Oak Lawn Ave., Dallas 75219; (214) 219-8588.

"I LOVE the designer resale stores. I love to buy things there that I couldn't afford when I first saw them on Rodeo Drive."

—SHAY CUNLIFFE, COSTUME DESIGNER FOR *ENOUGH*

SIDE TRIP: HOUSTON

VINTAGE

Buffalo Exchange: 1614 Westheimer Rd., Houston 77006; (713) 523-8701.

Pin Pin Vintage Clothing Store: 2538 Times Blvd., Houston 77005; (713) 520-9156.

Vintage Oasis: 1512 Westheimer Rd., Houston 77006; (713) 529-2234.

Way We Wore: 2602 Waugh Dr., Houston 77006; (713) 526-8910.

DESIGNER RESALE

Anew-U-Ladies Resale: 13147 Northwest Fwy. # 130, Houston 77040; (713) 462-6398.

Another Debut: 1432 FM 1960 Rd. West, Houston 77073; (281) 440-4050.

Arlynea & Arfele's Red Door: 2532 Nottingham St., Houston 77005; (713) 522-4343.

Baubles & Beads Resale Boutique: 3503 W. Holcombe Blvd., Houston 77025; (713) 592-5501 and 110 FM 1960 Rd. West, Houston 77090; (281) 537-2223.

Best Little Wearhouse In Texas: 6415 San Felipe St. # J, Houston 77057; (713) 334-9327.

Blue Bird Circle: 615 W. Alabama St., Houston 77006; (713) 528-0470.

Check My Closet: 10782 Grant Rd., Houston 77070; (281) 955-0806.

Hand Me Downs: 5257 Buffalo Speedway, Houston 77005; (713) 660-7434.

Nearly New Shop: 18093 Upper Bay Rd., Houston 77058; (281) 333-4497.

Style Plus Consignment: 4860 Beechnut St., Houston 77096; (713) 349-8001.

Twice New: 2005 W. Gray St. #D, Houston 77019; (713) 523-2212.

LARGER THAN LIFE-RUBENESQUE RESALE

$

10233 E. Northwest Hwy. #435, Dallas 75238; (214) 342-8550.
Open Tues–Sat: 10 a.m.–6 p.m., Thurs: 10 a.m.–8 p.m.
www.largerdallas.com

Owner: Kat Krone and Bencey Bryan
Return Policy: All sales final
Try-on Facilities: Two large private dressing rooms with large mirrors

Larger Than Life-Rubenesque Resale is run by mother-and-daughter team Krone and Bryan, who personally shopped resale "until we got too fat." So they opened this exclusively plus-sized consignment shop (after being fired from different jobs on the same day). "Something was telling us it was time to open our own shop," they joke. Seven years later they are still the only exclusively plus-sized consignment shop in Dallas.

Periwinkle walls display vintage gloves and purses and house their collection of Elizabeth, Ellen Tracy, Kaspar, and Carole Little. Current store inventory includes: a "Jerry Lewis" size 4X red faux fox coat; "We Be Bop" patchwork, batik rayon shirts in a rainbow of colors and in sizes 2X–6X; and a stylish Jones New York brown and cream silk and rayon herringbone suit. Krone personally collects WW II home front sweetheart jewelry.

Additional Resale Stores

Clothes Circuit Decidedly Upscale Resale: 6105 Sherry Ln., Dallas 75225; (214) 696-8634.

Dot's Closet: 5812 Live Oak St., Dallas 75214; (214) 826-4099.

Gift Horse at Clotheshorse Anonymous: 1413 Preston Forest Sq., Dallas 75230; (972) 233-7005.

Labels Designer Resale: 18101 Preston Rd. #A105, Dallas 75252; (972) 713-7470.

My Secret Closet, Inc.: 17194 Preston Rd. #118, Dallas 75248; (972) 267-1144.

Rethreads: 12835 Preston Rd. Ste. 411, Dallas 75230; (972) 233-9323.

Revente-Upscale Resale: 5400 E. Mockingbird Ln. #113, Dallas 75206; (214) 823-2800.

Robin Hood Designer Resale: 6609 Hillcrest Ave. #A, Dallas 75205; (214) 360-9666.

NEW ORLEANS

FUNKY MONKEY

$–$$

3127 Magazine St., New Orleans 70115; (504) 899-5587.
Open Mon–Sat: 11 a.m.–6 p.m., Sun: noon–5 p.m.

> *Owner:* Sarah Wheelock
> *Return Policy:* All vintage sales final
> *Try-on Facilities:* Three dressing rooms with mirrors

Funky Monkey's owner, Sarah Wheelock, an avid thrifter, has been in business for only six years but is already expanding to a second floor with more merchandise and dressing rooms. At first she carried only vintage clothing, but New Orleans being the party city it is, she started adding costumes from local designers as well as items such as wigs and sunglasses. "Though Mardi Gras and Halloween are the two big dress up times, people here dress up year round," says Wheelock. One of her local designers makes wonderfully decadent costumes, some mythologically or historically inspired, others with a Moulin Rouge feel.

This cheerful, bright store is painted bright yellow with a red floor. It features a policy of buy-sell-exchange, particularly welcomed by their college-age clientele.

TRASHY DIVA

$$–$$$

829 Chartres St., New Orleans 70116; (504) 581-4555.
Open Daily: noon–6 p.m.
www.trashydiva.com or www.victoriancorsets.com

> *Owner:* Candice Gwinn and Robyn Lewis
> *Return Policy:* Store sales final
> *Try-on Facilities:* Two dressing rooms with a huge eight-foot mirror

Trashy Diva sells vintage clothing and contemporary clothing with vintage appeal in a "Victorian revival shop" complete with crystal chandeliers. Gathered from around the world, designers include Isabella Costumiere and Sue Nice corsets, 1920s–40s cocktail and eveningwear, vintage-style stockings, crinolines, pettipants, vintage and vintage-style lingerie, ostrich boas, costume jewelry (both modern and vintage), and handbags.

"We most recently have expanded our collections to include our own Trashy Diva line of clothing," says Gwinn. "Our pieces are vintage inspired using only fine fabrics. Most of the pieces have a distinct 1920s–40s feeling. The wonderful thing about our pieces is that they are not reproduction but are modern sizes and shapes with great vintage details: covered buttons, smocking, ruching, gathering, and ruffles."

The most interesting items owners Gwinn and Lewis have collected include a hat and bag owned by Joan Crawford; a dress owned by Bette Davis; and a mysterious hand-painted kimono coat, adorned with ladies faces, that was rumored to have belonged to Hedy Lamarr. Their favorite periods are the '20s and '30s for "great prints and soft, flowing fabrics. How could you not love elaborate beading and laces that are virtually impossible to produce today?"

Current offerings include: a black, '20s, Asian-inspired, beaded silk chiffon flapper dress covered in an elaborate beaded pattern of oriental vases and flowers; and a Trashy Diva button dress, the hands down favorite dress from their line. This black silk georgette dress features cap sleeves, full front gathers, an empire waist, and a hemline that falls below the knee. Based on original Victorian corsets down to the steel boning, their Isabella corsets cinch the waist an average of 4–5 inches with back lacing ribbons. The fabrics range from menswear-inspired pinstripes to Chinese brocades.

 ELLEN BARKIN wore a lace, beaded, black vintage tunic she purchased 20 years ago to the 2000 *Vanity Fair* Oscar party.

Additional Vintage Stores

Gerald D. Katz Antiques: 505 Royal St., New Orleans 70130; (504) 524-5050.

Ragin' Daisy Vintage: 3125 Magazine St., New Orleans 70115; (504) 269-1960.

DESIGNER RESALE

THE ENCORE SHOPPE

$–$$

7814 Maple St., New Orleans 70118; (504) 861-9028.
Open Tues–Sat: 11 a.m.–4 p.m.

Owner: Louisiana Philharmonic Orchestra Volunteers
Return Policy: All sales final
Try-on Facilities: Three dressing rooms with mirrors

The Encore Shoppe is owned and operated as a fundraiser for the Louisiana Philharmonic Orchestra. Located in a lovely Victorian cottage, this store showcases Escada, St. John Knits, designer suits, cocktail dresses, evening gowns, plus shoes and accessories. Open for more than 35 years, The Encore Shoppe has a mix of high-end to bridgewear merchandise for all ages. Since some of their items are donated and their sales staff volunteers, they are able to offer exceptionally good prices.

"It is important when shopping to know who you are and to not wear anything you wouldn't wear if it was bought brand new and current. Otherwise, the clothes will wear you."

—MICHAEL KAPLAN, COSTUME DESIGNER FOR *PEARL HARBOR*

ON THE OTHER HAND

$–$$

8126 Hampson St., New Orleans 70118; (504) 861-0159.
Open Mon–Sat: 10 a.m.–6 p.m.

Owner: Kay Danné
Return Policy: All sales final
Try-on Facilities: Four dressing rooms with mirrors

On the Other Hand, a 3,000-square-foot store located in the River Bed art community of New Orleans, has been in business since 1987 and receives clothes from around the world, sent from customers who first found Danné's store as New Orleans tourists. She features high-end labels such as Michael Kors, Fendi, and Louis Vuitton, as well as resortwear, designer jeans, accessories, and shoes. "Designer resale is a great way to recoup your fashion dollars and shop couture with no pangs of guilt," says Danné. "Why pay the original retail for unused Chanel boots, when you can have them for less than a third of the cost?"

There is a large selection of ball gowns, "New Orleans being second only to Washington, D.C. in the sale of ball gowns per capita; also wedding gowns, including Vera Wang; and custom-made gowns from around the world." Danné offers a limited selection of vintage, including furs.

On the Other Hand offers a patio with hammocks, wine, and cheese, for husbands to enjoy while their wives shop. On Saturdays there is even live piano music.

"I mix thrift store items such as fake fur jackets with basic pieces from retail chain stores. Resale shops are great places for finding designer pieces that you can incorporate into your wardrobe."

—LINDA SERIJAN-FASMER, COSTUME DESIGNER FOR *FELICITY*

PRIMA DONNA'S CLOSET

$$–$$$

1218 Saint Charles Ave., New Orleans 70130; (504) 525-3327.
Open Mon–Sat: 10 a.m.–6 p.m.

Owner: Stephanie Hirsh
Return Policy: Case by case basis
Try-on Facilities: Dressing room

Prima Donna's Closet's owner Hirsh comes from a 25-year background in
the retail fashion business and brings an elegant boutique style, where customer service is paramount, to her three stores. She enthusiastically loves
both her clients and customers and believes in building relationships. Hirsh
carries the treasures of largely better labels such as Chanel, Guy Laroche, and
Anne Klein; however, she also carries lots of the younger lines such as BCBG
to satisfy her twentysomething clientele, who look for both current "trendy"
and classic looks. Hirsh also caters to larger women in her Metairie store,
with sizes 0–26, and in her new store at 1206 Saint Charles.

Also at 1206 Saint Charles Ave., New Orleans 70130; (504) 525-3327.
4409 Chastant St., Metairie 70006; (504) 885-3327.

Additional Resale Stores

Designers Konnection: 2549 Banks St., New Orleans 70119;
(504) 822-2229.

"What I admire is not fashion, it's clothes. A classic
Chanel jacket is not fashion; it's part of history."

—FRANCO MOSCHINO

CHICago

BEATNIX

$$

3400 N. Halsted St., Chicago 60657; (773) 281-6933.
Open Daily: 10 a.m.–midnight.

Owner: Keith Bucceri
Return Policy: All sales final
Try-on Facilities: Dressing room with mirror

Beatnix specializes in fun, "costumey" clothing, but they sell new clothing if it's "club oriented." Twenty years ago this boutique sold only vintage, but now it offers a wide variety of styles. Owner Bucceri's personal collection of Claire McCardell dresses "should be in a museum," and his favorite pieces are Kenneth Lane and William Spratling jewelry. Bucceri boasts a beautiful Schiaparelli ocelot coat in mint condition that he parted with for a mere $800.

Beatnix's merchandise comes and goes quickly. They get thousands of items each week, including '70s Pucci and Givenchy.

LOST ERAS/
A LOST ERA COSTUMES

$$

1515 W. Howard St., Chicago 60626; (773) 764-7400.
Open Mon–Sat: 10 a.m.–6 p.m. or by appointment.
www.alostera.com.

Owner: Charlotte Walters
Return Policy: All sales final
Try-on Facilities: Well-lit fitting rooms with mirrors

Lost Eras/A Lost Era Costumes is like stepping back into a lost era; it's an elegant boutique with vintage display cases and décor that offers unique and unusual clothing. Owner Walters believes that one-of-a-kind items are the most beautiful and add a feeling of class and glamour to your life. Her favorite period is the Elizabethan Renaissance with its beautiful, intricate metals; jewelry; and beadwork, which look very Victorian.

Current offerings include a mint-condition, camel-colored wool coat with fur trim from the '40s.

ROADKING

$$$

1024 N. Western Ave., Chicago 60622; (773) 486-1004.
Open Daily: noon–9 p.m.

Owner: Paul and Christine Kopko
Return Policy: Fourteen day exchange
Try-on Facilities: Dressing room with mirrors

Roadking specializes in American- and European-made vintage leather with labels such as Vanson and Aero. Step into their "industrial motorcycle motif" store for the "best selection of vintage and horsehide motoring apparel in the Midwest," says Kopko. Their favorite periods are the 1930s–50s because of their quality. Their personal collection includes: a 1920s horsehide Harley-Davidson motorcycle jacket; an Indian Ranger jacket from 1949 (the only year they were made); and a 1946 jewel-studded, D-pocket, horsehide Buco with original documentation of purchase.

Current offerings include: a size 46, black, 1952 Buco horsehide racer; a Lewis Leathers racing suit worn by R. J. Reynolds; a 1930s New York three-quarter horsehide police coat; and a 1940s horsehide Kit Carson autographed by the rock band The Reverend Horton Heat. Roadking's merchandise was in a ZZ Top video.

SHANGRI-LA
$$

1952 W. Roscoe St., Chicago 60657; (773) 348-5090.
Open Mon–Sat: noon–7 p.m., Sun: noon–5 p.m.

Owner: Debbie Gallo
Return Policy: All sales final
Try-on Facilities: Two dressing rooms

Shangri-La is small but brightly decorated and packed with goodies from estate sales and flea markets, including designers Pucci, Lilly Pulitzer, Givenchy, and Schiaparelli. Mainly offering affordable, casual, everyday vintage, Shangri-La primarily sells styles from the 1940s–70s; their best items are '60s and '70s, and they are currently carrying some '80s items.

One of their most interesting pieces, according to Gallo, is a blue and white, wool gabardine Western shirt and pants set, festooned with fringe, rhinestones, and embroidery, and custom-made in New York for a country performer. Gallo personally collects '30s silk, velvet gowns, but for the store she likes to find the brightest, wildest '60s and '70s pieces—her "crazy patterned" polyester shirts are big sellers.

Current offerings include: a '70s black web-look polyester jumpsuit with lace-up front, sides, and huge bell-bottoms; an '80s red leather "Thriller" jacket ("just like Michael Jackson's"); and a variety of Lilly Pulitzer skirts and pants.

Barbra Streisand wore an antique 1860 necklace of Burmese rubies to the 2002 Oscars. According to columnist Liz Smith, she has owned this necklace for years and designed the rest of her ensemble around it. The rubies came first, then a burgundy velvet skirt and top were added, and finally a wrap from an antique length of crushed velvet.

VINTAGE

Minneapolis Ragstock Co.: 1433 W. Lake St., Minneapolis 55408; (612) 823-6690.

Moejo's Clothes: 2040 Marshall Ave., St. Paul 55104; (651) 647-5700.

One More Tyme: 1839 E. 38th St., Minneapolis 55407; (612) 724-3222.

Repeat Performance Vintage: 3404 Lyndale Ave. South, Minneapolis 55408; (612) 824-3035.

Roses' Vintage: 1330 Grand Ave., St. Paul 55105; (651) 696-5242.

St. Paul Ragstock Co.: 1515 University Ave. West, St. Paul 55104; (651) 644-2733.

Tatters Clothing: 2928 Lyndale Ave. South, Minneapolis 55408; (612) 823-5285.

DESIGNER RESALE

Better Than Ever: 11 E. 58th St., Minneapolis 55419; (612) 861-7030.

Clothes Encounter of Plus Kind: 610 Selby Ave., St. Paul 55427; (651) 228-9424.

Down on 42nd Avenue: 7180 42nd Ave. North, Minneapolis 55427; (763) 537-3374.

Elite Repeat: 1336 Randolph Ave., St. Paul 55105; (651) 699-2315.

Encore Boutique: 242 Hamline Ave. South, St. Paul 55105; (651) 699-7522.

Nu Look Consignment Apparel: 4956 Penn Ave. South, Minneapolis 55409; (612) 925-0806.

Pink Closet: 4024 E. 46th St., Minneapolis 55406; (612) 724-2468.

SILVER MOON

$$

3337 N. Halsted St., Chicago 60657; (773) 883-0222.
Open Tues–Sun: noon–6 p.m.

Owner: Tari Costan
Return Policy: Case by case basis
Try-on Facilities: Dressing room with mirrors

Silver Moon is an upscale store that specializes in glamour such as evening gowns and men's tails from the 1800s–1950s. Costan also offers a large selection of men's suits from the 1940s–60s and a great deal of vintage designer clothing from the '20s and '30s such as gorgeous fringe shawls, cocktail dresses, '40s rayon dresses, men's fedoras, and top hats. Looking for a vintage wedding gown? Silver Moon offers wedding gowns from the 1900s–1960s. In addition, they stock a collection of '40s and '50s men's gabardine jackets.

Costan's favorite period is the 1900s–1940s because of the quality, design, and fabulous fabrics "unlike anything on the market today." One of her favorites? A black velvet coat from the '30s, decorated with rhinestones that "make it look like the sky" with pointed, dropped sleeves that hang down to the floor.

STUDIO V

$$

672 N. Dearborn St., Chicago 60610; (312) 440-1937.
Open Mon–Sat: noon–6 p.m., winter hours include Sun: 1 p.m.–5 p.m.
www.studiovchicago.com

Owner: Sheldon Atovsky
Return Policy: All vintage sales final
Try-on Facilities: One dressing room with two full-length mirrors

Studio V (the "V" stands for "vintage") was founded in 1975 and has been in its present location since 1982, located four blocks west of Michigan Avenue, Chicago's prime retail center. They carry original and newly made fashions for men and women in art nouveau, art deco, and art moderne styles and are known for "terrific service and an eclectic mix of interesting merchandise at reasonable prices." Atovsky prefers the art deco period for its clean lines, sense of balance, and imaginative designs.

Current offerings include: an extremely subtle and sophisticated painted poppy flower pendant; a 1940s mother of pearl and rhinestone mint minaudière; and a celluloid and hand-set rhinestone bangle with two peacock designs.

UNA MAE'S FREAK BOUTIQUE
$$

1422 N. Milwaukee Ave., Chicago 60622; (773) 276-7002.
Open Mon–Fri: noon–8 p.m., Sat: 11 a.m.–8 p.m., Sun: 11 a.m.–7 p.m.
www.unamaes.com

Owner: Karen Prendergast and Nancy Becker
Return Policy: Exchange/store credit only
Try-on Facilities: Two dressing rooms with full-length mirrors

Una Mae's Freak Boutique is a "creative, funky, colorful, cozy boutique specializing in vintage and new affordable threads and jewelry for men, women, rock stars, and geeks," say Prendergast and Becker. Why? "That's what we like." Una Mae's offers U.S. designers and imports from all over the world, including never-worn vintage patent leather '60s jackets and wool fish-embroidered Western jackets.

Their favorite period is the '40s because of the classic and classy cuts, the '60s for semi-casual clothes, and the '70s when "we want to be sexy. We love vintage, it's hard to have a favorite, though." Current offerings include: a '50s compact lighter/lipstick case with mother of pearl in pristine condition; tuxedo pants for men; and Peruvian scarves and hats.

WISTERIA

$$

3715 N. Southport Ave., Chicago 60613; (773) 880-5868.
Open Thurs/Fri: 4 p.m.–10 p.m., Sat: noon–9 p.m., Sun: noon–5 p.m.

> **Manager:** Jeff Koontz
> **Return Policy:** Case by case basis
> **Try-on Facilities:** Brightly colored dressing rooms

Wisteria is a vintage emporium of clothing and gifts, "setting the scene for swing, rockabilly, lounge, ballroom, disco, or a fabulous party." Wisteria has taken the art of recycling style to its highest level. Some of their star quality clothing has seen the silver screen in Woody Allen movies, been flaunted at local theatres like the Steppenwolf and Goodman, and has adorned actors of the Black Dance Ensemble. Julia Roberts, Cameron Diaz, Dillon McDermott, and locals like Will Klinger (of Wild Chicago) have shopped at Wisteria.

Most of the clothing items come from local original owners. Wisteria specializes in period clothing prior to 1970, with a big emphasis on the '40s, '50s, and '60s. They specialize in cocktail dresses, tuxedos, hats, scarves, lingerie, sharkskin suits, jewelry, day dresses, ties, smoking jackets, and overcoats.

Additional Vintage Stores

A.L. Sacluti Sales: 3039 West Carroll Ave., Chicago 60612; (773) 265-0100.

Arrow: 1452 W. Chicago Ave., Chicago 60622; (312) 738-2755.

Hubba-Hubba: 3309 N. Clark St., Chicago 60657; (773) 477-1414.

Ragstock Stores: 812 W. Belmont Ave. 2nd Floor, Chicago 60657; (773) 868-9263.

Strange Cargo: 3448 N. Clark St., Chicago 60657; (773) 327-8090.

Threads Etc.: 2327 N. Milwaukee Ave., Chicago 60647; (773) 276-6411.

SIDE TRIP: CINCINNATI

VINTAGE

Casablanca Vintage: 3944 Spring Grove Ave., Cincinnati 45223;
(513) 541-6999.

Down Town Nostalgic: 119 Calhoun St., Cincinnati 45219;
(513) 861-9336.

Gayle's Vintage Clothing: 3742 Kellogg Ave., Cincinnati 45226;
(513) 321-7341.

Talk of the Town: 9111 Reading Rd., Cincinnati 45215;
(513) 563-8844.

DESIGNER RESALE

Chaz Bridal & Consignment: 7333 Montgomery Rd., Cincinnati 45236;
(513) 791-4868.

Encore Resale & Consignment: 4888 Guerley Rd., Cincinnati 45238;
(513) 921-5204.

Impressions II Consignment Boutique: 3803 Harrison Ave.,
Cincinnati 45211; (513) 662-8300.

Jean A Faye Consignments: 8314 Plainfield Rd., Cincinnati 45236;
(513) 891-2434.

More Than Clothes: 3502 Decoursey Ave., Covington 41015;
(859) 581-4131.

Peacock Clothing Consignments: 3048 Madison Rd., Cincinnati
45209; (513) 396-6464.

Underground Treasures: 1727 Galbraith Ave., Cincinnati 45215;
(513) 728-4192.

Vintage Fiber Works: 1869 N. Damen Ave., Chicago 60647;
(773) 862-6070.

Wacky Cats: 3012 N. Lincoln Ave., Chicago 60657; (773) 929-6701.

Additional Resale Stores

Bella Moda Consignment House: 947 N. State St., Chicago 60610;
(312) 642-0300.

Big Pay Back: 1329 S. Michigan Ave., Chicago 60605; (312) 588-0199.

Chatham Resale Shop: 645 E. 79th St., Chicago 60619; (773) 483-0574.

The Daisy Shop: 67 E. Oak St. 6th Floor, Chicago 60611;
(312) 943-8880.

Designer Resale of Chicago, Inc.: 658 N. Dearborn St., Chicago 60610;
(312) 587-3312.

Duomo Men's Designer Resale: 2906 N. Broadway St., Chicago 60657;
(773) 325-2325.

Elliotts Consignment Store: 2465 N. Lincoln Ave., Chicago 60614;
(773) 404-6080; and 3015 N. Broadway St., Chicago 60657;
(773) 549-4330.

McShane's Exchange: 815 W. Armitage Ave., Chicago 60614;
(773) 525-0282.

A Woman's Consignment Shop: 1141 W. Webster Ave., Chicago 60614;
(773) 525-0211.

SIDE TRIP: CLEVELAND

VINTAGE

Chelsea's Vintage Clothing: 1412 W. 116th St., Cleveland 44102; (216) 226-9147.

Cleveland Shop: 11606 Detroit Ave., Cleveland 44102; (216) 228-9725.

Legacy Antiques & Vintage: 12502 Larchmere Blvd., Cleveland 44120; (216) 229-0578.

Lorain Suite Antiques: 7105 Lorain Ave., Cleveland 44102; (216) 281-1959.

Off My Back: 26131 Detroit Rd., Cleveland 44145; (440) 835-8555.

Renaissance Parlour: 1838 1/2 Coventry Rd., Cleveland 44118; (216) 932-8840.

Seamonkeys: 13369 Madison Ave., Cleveland 44107; (216) 226-7901.

DESIGNER RESALE

Closets Consignment Boutique: 1100 Linda St., Cleveland 44116; (440) 333-5379.

Couture Club: 19034 Detroit Rd., Cleveland 44116; (440) 356-8945.

 Jamie Lee Curtis wore a white, beaded vintage dress that was previously owned by Marlene Dietrich and was given to Cutris by Maria Riva, Dietrich's daughter.

TORONTO

ACME RAG CO.

$

36 Kensington Ave., Toronto M5T 2J9; (416) 599-4220.
Open Mon–Sat: noon–6 p.m., Sun: noon–5 p.m.

Owner: Soosie Johnston
Return Policy: Case by case basis
Try-on Facilities: Dressing rooms

Acme Rag Co. is located in the fascinating, vibrant multi-ethnic area of Kensington Market, near downtown Toronto. Johnston has been in business for seven years and in that time has seen her customers change from teenagers scouting for T-shirts to 30- and 40-year-olds looking for more upscale items.

Soosie says what's hot changes quickly. Last year it was '60s and '70s clothing, and anything Pucci or Pucci-like. Right now studded and tooled chunky leather belts are big, as well as purses—whether designer or just funky. Strappy shoes and mules also sell well. Her store is small and cozy but has a friendly feel, and her merchandise is clean, fun, and well-priced.

> "My clothes are not a façade. They have an inner life."
> —GEOFFREY BEENE

BLACK MARKET VINTAGE CLOTHING & COLLECTIBLES

$

319 Queen St. West, Toronto M5V 2A4; (416) 599-5858.
Open Mon–Thurs and Sat: 11 a.m.–7 p.m., Fri: 10 a.m–8 p.m.,
Sun: 11 a.m.–6 p.m.

Owner: John Christman, Tracey Opperman, and Bernard Chung
Return Policy: Exchange within 14 days
Try-on Facilities: Several, including an old converted church confessional!

Black Market Vintage Clothing & Collectibles, located in a basement down a dark staircase, stocks inexpensive pants, jeans, leather jackets, shirts, and T-shirts. Décor consists of exposed pipes and irreverent references to the mainstream world of fashion such as pictures of camouflage designer T-shirts with inexpensive camouflage tank tops right next to them. Their customers are "tired of the media saturation and advertising on their clothes, and so are in search of T-shirts from the past, one of a kind. Once your mother finds it in the mall and gives it to you for Christmas, it's over!"

A second Black Market Vintage store is directly across the street, up a flight of stairs painted in black and purple swirls. This store has similar merchandise in a brighter but still irreverent setting. This vintage shop is not for lovers and collectors of fine things from the past but for the young. As one salesperson so aptly explained, "People have to have clothes, man!"

After 18 years in the business, Christman, Opperman, and Chungs' favorite pieces are too numerous to mention! But include lots of "original Levi's denim and costume pieces." Their favorite period "still has to be the '60s and '70s for the colorful wackiness of it all. But we're partial to any decade with a sense of humor and fun, like the '80s."

WINONA RYDER wore the same vintage Pauline Trigère gown to the 2000 Oscars that the late Trigère had worn to pick up her first design award in 1949. As a Best Supporting Actress '94 Oscar nominee for *The Age of Innocence*, Ryder wore a vintage, white, beaded 1959 Edward Sebesta gown.

"Good vintage means anything that can come clean and not disintegrate on wearing. Good value means buyer beware. High prices don't necessarily mean perfect condition."

—MOLLY MAGINNIS, COSTUME DESIGNER FOR
AS GOOD AS IT GETS AND *TALES OF THE CITY*

BRAVA

$

483 Queen St. West, Toronto M5V 2A9; (416) 504-8742.
Open Mon–Sat: 10:30 a.m.–7:30 p.m., Sun: 1 p.m.–6 p.m.

Owner: Jeanette Shanks
Return Policy: Case by case basis
Try-on Facilities: Changing rooms

Brava's merchandise is decidedly more "vintage" than just old, and the store features a rack of beautiful rayon 1940s dresses in perfect condition, a number of 1950s cocktail dresses, and some outrageous plaid, patchwork golf pants from the '70s. For men there are the ever popular Hawaiian shirts, some ties, and suede and leather jackets (almost a staple of every vintage store). Owner Jeanette Shanks has been in the business since the early '70s, though she started out in the antique market and says vintage fashions will always be popular even though tastes change. Now she sells lots of 1960s mod shirts with long collars, dresses for proms, and clothes for theme parties. She also sells to costume designers for film and stage.

CABARET NOSTALGIA

$$$

672 Queen St. West, Toronto M6J 1E5; (416) 504-7126.
Open Mon–Wed and Sat: 11 a.m.–6 p.m., Thurs/Fri: 11 a.m.–7 p.m.,
Sun: 1 p.m.–5 p.m.

Owner: Thomas Drayton
Return Policy: Exchange/store credit within two weeks with receipt
and tag attached
Try-on Facilities: Two changing rooms with mirrors

Cabaret Nostalgia makes an immediate, lovely first impression. The moment you walk in and hear the gentle sounds of classic jazz, you know you're in the presence of elegance and style. Drayton, whose mother and sister were also vintage collectors, has been collecting for 25 years. The store mainly carries items from the 1920s–50s. Many of the dresses have names, such as "Peach Parfait" and "Green with Envy," and there is everything from a spectacular Dior cocktail coat to a wide array of dresses ('40s rayon, '50s cocktail, and summer). Drayton says his 1930s wedding gowns are also popular.

For men there are tuxedos, smoking jackets, top hats, and bowlers. Downstairs holds even more treasures, including a baby's christening dress, fur coats, and a red 1930s opera coat. This store is obviously aimed at people who like dressing up. "Brooke Shields is a regular customer," says Drayton.

"People are not dressing up in real life," says assistant Elizabeth, "so they are finding occasions like theme parties and swing dance parties to do so." The most interesting piece collected is an Edwardian blouse—very Moulin Rouge, with ruffled sleeves—hung on the wall but sadly not for sale.

CIRCA FORTY INC.

$

456 Queen St. West, Toronto M5V 2A8; (416) 504-0880.
Open Mon–Sat: 11 a.m.–7 p.m., Sun: 11 a.m.–6 p.m.

Owner: Phil Apban
Return Policy: Exchange only
Try-on Facilities: Two changing rooms with mirrors outside

Circa Forty Inc. used to be a '40s boutique, but Apban wanted to have something to offer everyone, so this art deco store now offers vintage pieces through the '60s and '70s. Apban still loves the '40s but will not hold on to a piece because "money is more important than a garment." According to Apban, Bruce Springstein has shopped here.

COURAGE MY LOVE
$–$$

14 Kensington Ave., Toronto MST 2J7; (801) 979-1992.
Open Mon–Sat: 11:30 a.m.–6 p.m., Sun: 2 p.m.–5 p.m.

Owners: Pat Ray, Stewart Scriver, and Cece Scriver
Return Policy: All sales final
Try-on Facilities: Two dressing rooms

Courage My Love owners Scriver, Scriver, and Ray are a family team and have lived in the Kensington area for 20 years. Even their 88-year-old grandmother is part of the act—her needlework expertise allows her to repair antique lingerie, cashmere sweaters, and Victorian pieces to nearly perfection.While doing appraisals for the Royal Ontario Museum, the Scrivers began rescuing and restoring antiques that had been cast off as garbage. They quit both occupations to open Courage My Love and to travel frequently to Mexico, Thailand, Indonesia, and India in search of unique items for their artistic and eclectic store.

Authentic vintage pieces are plentiful, and they have supplied many films, including 300 men's suits and 500 hats for *A Christmas Story*. Their selection of '40s lingerie and kimonos is wonderful and they offer a wide array of vintage buttons. They also remake a lot of vintage pieces, transforming '40s and '50s tablecloths into purses, embellishing vintage T-shirts, and converting entire summer wardrobes into winter clothing.

"We just carry what we love," says Scriver, "because we really want people to think for themselves when they shop. With vintage and remade clothes people can express themselves as individuals."

CAMERON DIAZ carried a vintage Fred Leighton clutch and belted her Emanuel Ungaro dress with a vintage 19th-century Indian necklace, also from Fred Leighton, to the 2002 Oscars.

DIVINE DECADENCE

$$

136 Cumberland St. (upstairs), Toronto M5R 1A6; (877) 295-0299.
Open Mon–Thurs: noon–6 p.m., Fri: noon–7 p.m. or by appointment.
www.toronto.com/divinedecadence

Owner: Carmelita Blondet and Ivan Brugne
Return Policy: Exchange only
Try-on Facilities: Two changing rooms with mirrors outside

Devine Decadence has been owned by Blondet and Brugne for 30 years. Blondet, author of *Bringing Vintage to the Millenium*, was born and raised in Lima, Peru. Her Spanish mother (who "always dresses beautifully") and grandmother taught Blondet to cherish antiques, uphold tradition, and appreciate beautiful fabrics. The shop offers "vintage with a contemporary feel to best meet modern needs but in as authentic a way as possible," says Blondet. Favorite period? "I love the late '50s, the '30s bias cut, the *Breakfast at Tiffany's* look, anything feminine. I love sleek lines. A dress should be part of a woman, the flow of her body lines and such."

They carry designers from 1890 through the 1960s, stock from Paris and Italy, shawls from Peru, '60s silk chiffon, and bridal gowns. Current stock includes: a Victorian lace dress; a '50s lace and silk chiffon dress; and a '70s beaded lace dress. More unusual is their selection of linen garments, all hand-washed in organic soap. And they rebead garments and handbags. "Renée Zellweger, Lauren Hutton, and Milla Jovovich have shopped here."

"The reality of dressing today is that a woman will wear a jacket she bought last year with a five-year-old pullover and today's skirt. Part of being modern is the choice of how to put yourself together."

—GIORGIO ARMANI

159

THE PAPER BAG PRINCESS
$$$$

287 Davenport Rd. Toronto M5R 1J9
Open Tues–Sat: noon–7 p.m.
www.ThePaperBagPrincess.com

Owner: Elizabeth M. Mason
Return Policy: All sales final
Try-on facilities: Unknown at press time

The Paper Bag Princess is Toronto-born Elizabeth Mason's satellite location of her highly successful Los Angeles boutique. Known internationally as one of the top experts in high-end vintage couture, and supplier of many of the vintage gowns worn by celebrities, Mason hopes to repeat her success in her hometown. Author of two books, her latest publication is Valuable Vintage, a guide to pricing and collecting important vintage fashions. The store is scheduled to open September 2002 and promises to be an exciting addition to Toronto's vintage and resale market.

DESIGNER RESALE

ACT TWO
$–$$$

596 Mount Pleasant Rd., Toronto M4S 2M6; (416) 487-2486.
Open Mon–Sat: 11 a.m.–6 p.m.

Owner: Inga Weisman
Return Policy: All sales final
Try-on Facilities: Three changing rooms with mirrors

Act Two's vivacious owner, Inga Weisman, offers high-end designer resale and a selection of vintage in a 322-square-foot boutique with yellow walls and forest green shelves. Weisman specializes in European men's and women's designers because "I grew up with it…Demeulemeester for the cut and materials, Martine Sitbon for details, Armani and Chanel for salability, Versace for glamour, and vintage for the beauty and novelty. My love is also for Issey Miyake's wool sweaters, skirts, and suits and Yohji Yamamoto and Rei Kawakubo because I love the structure, which is like architecture." Weisman is friendly, knowledgeable, and loves the labels only if the garments are made of fine fabrics. Among the most interesting pieces in her personal collection are a Chanel cocktail dress from 1950 and a 1980s Yohji Yamamoto lab coat.

Weisman now carries many garments left over from films shot in Toronto, including some wonderful evening gowns and sportswear worn by Jennifer Love Hewitt; some even bear the actress' name inside. Act Two's clothing has also been seen in *The Hurricane* with Denzel Washington and *Forever Mine* with Gretchen Mol.

L'Elegante Ltd.

$$$

122 Yorkville Ave., Toronto M5R 1C2; (416) 923-3220.
Open Mon–Wed and Fri/Sat: 10 a.m.–6 p.m., Thurs: 10 a.m.–7 p.m.,
Sun: 11 a.m.–5 p.m.

Owner: Dee Houghton
Return Policy: Case by case basis
Try-on Facilities: Dressing rooms

L'Elegante Ltd. is an upscale resale store located in the Toronto are of Yorkville, which was developed in the '60s. The area now houses a collection of chic restaurants, boutiques, pubs, cafés, and antique stores. Merchandise is nicely organized but definitely on the high end of the resale market.

Owner Dee Houghton is the great niece of the first owner of L'Elegante, Mary Gauvreau, a Toronto socialite who started the business 29 years ago. Houghton opened a second location 8 years ago. Why does Houghton love resale so much? "It just makes sense, no matter how you look at it," says Houghton. "Classic, quality clothing doesn't wear out."

Houghton's customers come from the world over—women in the work force who travel internationally always visit her when in Toronto, and her consignors also find her from overseas; she currently has several from England and Switzerland.

Businesswear is her biggest seller, but eveningwear also sells well because "women in Toronto are dressing up to go out in the evening." Hats are popular for both summer and winter along with quality costume jewelry, shoes, purses, and pashmina shawls. What sells best? "Chanel just flies out the door."

Also at 1900 Dundas St. West, Mississauga M6R 3B6; (905) 822-9610.

EX-TOGGERY STORES
$

1640 Avenue Rd., Toronto M5M 3X9; (416) 781-0734.
Open Mon/Tues and Sat: 10 a.m.–6 p.m., Wed–Fri: 10 a.m.–9 p.m.,
Sun: noon–5 p.m.

Owner: Michael Allen
Return Policy: Refund on full price merchandise within 24 hours
Try-on Facilities: Dressing rooms

Ex-Toggery debunks the notion that secondhand stores are here today and gone tomorrow. This business was started in 1939 by the present owner's grandfather. Bright and well-organized, it carries average and serviceable clothes—not a "Lagerfeld, Boss, Armani" collection. However, you can't beat good, clean everyday clothes in all sizes at very low prices, which are discounted 20 percent after four weeks and 50 percent after six weeks.

One has to look hard for the real treasures, though in the men's section, Eden found a beautiful Ermenegildo Zegna navy blazer with hand-stitched lapels—and for a song.

KATIE'S CONSIGNMENT

$$

94 George St., Oakville L6J 3B7; (905) 845-9996.
Open Tues–Sat: 10:30 a.m.–5 p.m.

Owner: Katie Carrigg
Return Policy: All sales final
Try-on Facilities: Three dressing rooms

Katie's Consignment has been at this location just outside Toronto for eight years. Carrigg does a great deal of business by phone since she knows her customers well and calls them when something "just right" comes in. She carries Nipon, Versace, and Escada, along with the well-known Canadian designer Wayne Clarke. She thinks Americans are more flamboyant and Canadians more conservative but quickly adds, "Don't get me wrong. I'm very proud to be a Canadian."

PREVIOUSLY LOVED DESIGNER CLOTHING

$$

986 Bathurst St., Toronto M5R 3G6; (416) 516-3613.
Open Mon–Sat: 10:30 a.m.–5:30 p.m.

Owner: Barb Davis
Return Policy: Within two weeks with receipt
Try-on Facilities: Dressing room

Previously Loved Designer Kids Clothing also stocks high-end and designer clothing for women and specializes in European (mostly French and Italian) designers. "I have a very specific client base that is looking for beautiful, expensive, unique clothing at a greatly reduced price," says Davis.

SECOND NATURE BOUTIQUE

$$–$$$

514 Mount Pleasant Rd., Toronto M4S 2M2; (416) 481-4924.
Open Mon–Sat: 10 a.m.–6 p.m.

Owner: Ruth Silverberg and Kary Dick
Return Policy: Refund within 24 hours
Try-on Facilities: Four fitting rooms on main floor, one on lower level, private curtained one on third level

Second Nature Boutique owners Silverberg and Dick, a mother-and-daughter team, offer "small racks and big designers, such as Betsey Johnson, Versace, Prada, Dolce & Gabbana, Armani, Chanel, Ralph Lauren, Louis Vuitton, and Anne Klein. We service a lot of high-profile women in business and the public eye."

Everything from casual to cocktail clothing to accessories is offered. "We cater to all ages; we sell clothing that will take you from weekends to work to evening. If we come across great vintage, we will take it."

The store was established in 1974 as a family-owned business. "Once you've shopped resale, you'll never do retail. We feel we are offering a service for all women. We give you the opportunity to be able to own designer clothing, add to your wardrobe, or try something new.

"We have a variety of purses to match our treasures—JP Tods, Prada, Louis Vuitton to name a few. We have many regular consignors as well as buyers. Our stock comes in every half hour, so every day is like walking into a new store. We have three floors; the upper level carries eveningwear by Betsey Johnson, Fendi, Prada, etc. On the main level are accessories, purses, jewelry, separates, suits, etc. The lower level is reduced items up to 70 percent off."

Current stock includes: a cream silk Chloé gown that is off the shoulder with hand-beaded pom-pom trim; a great assortment of Armani suits; designer capes; and lots of separates, both casual and cocktail, from Dolce & Gabanna, Fendi, and DKNY.

SHOPPE D'OR LIMITED

$$–$$$

18 Cumberland St., Toronto M4W 1J5; (416) 923-2384.
Open Mon–Sat: 10 a.m.–6 p.m.

Owner: Norma Victoria King-Wilson
Return Policy: Case by case basis
Try-on Facilities: Four dressing rooms with mirrors upstairs

Shoppe d'Or Limited spans two stories and stays bright and airy with a two-story bay window. The business was founded in 1947 by King-Wilson's grandmother, Vera Victoria Morrison, who was succeeded by her daughter Joy Donna King-Wilson in 1969, "then by me in 1980. We have always been in Yorkville." She carries everything, but the handbags (by such names as Chanel and Louis Vuitton) especially "go very quickly." King-Wilson sells about 20,000 pieces a year and says she never advertises. Her customers know the value of things, she maintains, and have already priced the items at full retail. "They are smart shoppers."

Additional Resale Stores

Sweet Repeats: 724 Annette St., Toronto M6S 2E2; (416) 763-0009.

MONTREAL

A LA DEUX

$$

316 Av du Mont-Royal E., Montréal H2T 1P7; (514) 843-4904.
Open Mon–Wed and Sat: 11 a.m.–6 p.m., Thurs/Fri: 11 a.m.–9 p.m.,
Sun: noon–5 p.m.

Owner: Jeannine Lussier
Return Policy: All sales final
Try-on Facilities: Three dressing rooms

A La Deux is a cozy store decorated with a comfortable sofa and old lampshades. Lussier often ships to Japan's younger set, who love the '70s. In her retail location, she is strong in the 1940s–70s for dresses, hats, purses, and accessories.

RETRO RAGZ RETRO RAGS

$

171 Av du Mont-Royal E., Montréal H2T 1P2; (514) 849 6181.
Open Sun–Wed: noon–6 p.m., Thurs/Fri: noon–9 p.m.

Owner: Jamie Etcovitch
Return Policy: Exchange only
Try-on Facilities: Three fitting rooms

Retro Ragz Retro Rags is a warm, casual, wonderfully bizarre store that offers inexpensive merchandise aimed at a young clientele. Specializing in the '70s, Etcovitch finds that polyester and Ban-Lon items are most popular, but he also sells lots of '70s track suits, flares, Western shirts, ski sweaters and jackets, Eskimo jackets with Inuit prints, and heavy suede coats with fur collars. Largely, but not exclusively, for women, he has been in business for ten years, and just opened his second store, Kitsch, right across the street.

Also at 164 Av du Mont-Royal E., Montréal H2T 1P1; (514) 982 9305.

Additional Vintage Stores

Folles Allieés: 365 Mont-Royal E., Montréal H2T 1R1; (514) 843-4904.

Malle Commode De Montréal: 760 Rue Rachel F Suite A, Montréal; (514) 521-9494.

Rose Nanan: 118 Mont-Royal E., Montréal H2T 1N8; (514) 289-9833.

"There's a feeling of independence attached to vintage dressing. Women...know there's a 99% chance that no one else will be wearing what they are wearing or more importantly, no one will have even seen it before."

—SUSAN CANNON, FASHION DIRECTOR, *JANE*

DESIGNER RESALE

BOUTIQUE ENCORE
$$$

2165 Crescent St., Montréal H3G 2C1; (514) 849-0092.
Open Tues–Fri: 10 a.m.–6 p.m., Sat: 10 a.m.–5 p.m.

Owner: Anna McKay
Return Policy: All sales final
Try-on Facilities: Dressing rooms

Boutique Encore is one of the oldest consignment stores in Canada. It opened 50 years ago on Sherbrooke Street, and moved to Crescent Street in 1995. This beautiful store is very upscale, organizing their racks into groups of designers. Versace, Emanuel Ungaro, Jean Paul Gaultier, Gucci, St. John, Issey Miyake, Chanel, and Gianfranco Ferre are a few of their must-have labels. Six years ago they added menswear and now sell suits and sportswear from Boss, Armani, Tommy Hilfiger, and Brioni at 25 to 50 percent off the original price.

Boutique Rose-Anne

$$$

1612 Rue Sherbrooke O., Montréal H3H 1C9; (514) 935-7960.
Open Tues–Fri: 10 a.m.–6 p.m., Sat: 10 a.m.–5 p.m.

Owner: Linda Silverman
Return Policy: All sales final
Try-on Facilities: Two dressing rooms

Boutique Rose-Anne is a charming store on the first and second floors of an old stone building. Children's wear is located on the first floor while the women's department is upstairs, full of suits from such designers as Escada, Guy Laroche, Donna Karan, Jean Paul Gaultier, Valentino, Jil Sander, Armani, and Gianfranco Ferre.

This eight-year-old store's new owner, Linda Silverman, has completely renovated the store with new paint, carpet, and decor. It is conveniently located near many of the big downtown hotels; customers are largely working women from offices nearby who want businesswear, sportswear, and eveningwear, especially evening suits. Chanel purses, always a favorite, are not on the floor, as customers on a waiting list are notified as soon as one arrives.

Le Rétroviseur

$

751 Rachel Est., Montréal M2J 2H4; (514) 528-1645.
Open Mon–Wed: noon–6 p.m., Thurs/Fri: noon–9 p.m.,
Sat/Sun: noon–5 p.m.

Owner: Ian Banfield
Return Policy: Within one week with receipt
Try-on Facilities: Two changing rooms

Le Rétroviseur, established in 1982, is located in a 100-year-old storefront building with hardwood floors and molded plaster ceilings. Offering both resale and vintage, they carry designers like Jacques & Koko, Anne Klein, Perry Ellis, Ralph Lauren, Jones New York, Victoria's Secret, Liz Claiborne, Mexx, Esprit, Gap, and Levi's. One of the most interesting pieces Banfield has collected is a bubble dress from the '50s.

Banfield stocks a "large variety of fine clothing of high-quality fabrics. The great demand among my clientele is for this class of clothing, and it is what I am most able to find. We have a lot of extra-large clothing for men and women."

MARIE-CLAUDE

$$

2261 Av Papineau, Montréal H2K 4JS; (514) 529-5859.
Open Mon–Wed: 11 a.m.–6 p.m., Thurs/Fri: 11 a.m.–9 p.m.,
Sat/Sun: 11 a.m.–5 p.m.

> *Owner:* Michel Duclos
> *Return Policy:* All sales final
> *Try-on Facilities:* Two dressing rooms

Marie-Claude is a 2500-square-foot store located in an old print shop. Its large beams, columns, and exposed pipes lend it extraordinary character. Men's and women's merchandise is well organized, and all major American and European designers are represented such as Versace, Dolce & Gabbana, Armani, Gianfranco Ferre, and Burberry, as well as Canadian designers Marie St. Pierre and Jean Claude Poitras. Duclos also has another store in Outremount that carries only women's clothes, like the classic and conservative lines of Escada and Chanel.

Also at 1118 Laurier West, Outremount H2V 2L4; (514) 278-4197.

PLEIN LES YEUX
$$

C.P. 47525 CSP Plateau Mont-Royal, Montréal H2H 2S8; (514) 524-4822.
Open Daily 11 a.m.–6 p.m.
www.PleinLesYeux.com

Owner: Odette L. Brosseau
Return Policy: Store credit only
Try-on Facilities: Dressing room

Plein Les Yeux specializes in accessories and stocks over 400–500 handbags, a wealth of gloves, and a smattering of hats packed into the shop. Though Brosseau's store used to be packed with a multitude of designer labels, Brosseau opted to concentrate on her loves—purses and gloves. Brosseau prides herself in offering items that "emphasize your personality, your style—this is my specialty."

Brosseau's favorite period is the 1960s. "Black and white dresses, A-line skirts by Courrèges, and Guy Laroche's colored coats. My favorite designers are the divine Sonia Rykiel, Beretta, Kenzo, and Yamamoto."

VICE-VERSA FRIPE CHIC
$$

5175 C, rue Sherbrooke Ouest, Montréal H4A 1T5; (514) 369-7707.
Open Mon–Wed: 10 a.m.–6 p.m. or by appointment.

Owner: Linda Bensoussan
Return Policy: All sales final
Try-on Facilities: Three dressing rooms.

Vice-Versa Fripe Chic is a very personable, charming shop with chic, homestyle décor. Bensoussan offers resale and vintage clothing with designers such as Chanel, Armani, Versace, Valentino, and Pierre Balmain. She strongly believes in offering her clients the same personal services found in a haute couture boutique. "The Vice-Versa concept is not only a boutique for clothing and accessories but a place for professional fashion consultations and alteration. For Vice-Versa, fashion is self-expression."

Additional Resale Stores

Carrousel Pret-a-Porter: 343 Rue Fieury O., Montréal; (514) 389-8590.

Sarah Mode: 111 Rue Chabanel O. Ste. 721, Montréal H2N 1C8; (514) 385-3248.

Secret Bien Garde: 3463 Rue Robert-Chevalier, Montréal H1A 3R7; (514) 644-9527.

Via Mondo: 1103 Av Laurier O., Outrement, Montréal H2V 2L3; (514) 278-7334.

BOSTON

ABSOLUTELY FABULOUS

$$

108 Beacon St., Somerville 02143; (617) 864-0656.
Open Mon/Tues: noon–7 p.m., Wed–Fri: noon–8 p.m.,
Sat/Sun: 11 a.m.–7 p.m.

Owner: Collene Covey-Brien and Mara Kustra Loeber
Return Policy: Store credit within ten days
Try-on Facilities: Dressing room

Absolutely Fabulous is a funky, eclectic shop that carries clothing, hats, accessories, and jewelry, because "many stores are boring and our stuff will put some flare into everyone's style," says Covey-Brien. The owners specialize in the '50s and '60s, "elegant clothing cut to compliment every shape using fun, good quality fabric."

BOBBY FROM BOSTON

$$

19 Thayer St., Boston 02118; (617) 423-9299.
Open Mon–Sat: noon–6 p.m.

Owner: Bobby Garnett
Return Policy: Case by case basis
Try-on Facilities: Dressing room

Bobby From Boston is a dismantled and rebuilt men's store from 1922 that specializes in men's vintage from the Edwardian era to 1960. "Over the past five years, our business has been directed to the film industry, designers, and overseas wholesale (Europe and Asia). The business is very strong in vintage British menswear. Even though my favorite period visually is the 1930s," says Garnett, "I tend to wear more of the continental '60s, à la 007, Motown, and *The Avengers*." If you are not sure about wearing vintage, you can try it here without the commitment—they do rentals!

A celebrity amongst serious clothing collectors for his know-how and the sheer quantity of merchandise he has amassed, Garnett remains humble, attributing his love for style to his mother and their shopping excursions. Hollywood crosses the country for his wares and expertise, from dressing the extras for *Titanic* to supplying attire for TV's *That '70s Show*.

THE GARMENT DISTRICT INC.

$

200 Broadway, Cambridge 02139; (617) 876-5230.
Open Sun–Tues: 11 a.m.–7 p.m., Wed–Fri: 11 a.m.–8 p.m.,
Sat: 9 a.m.–7 p.m.
www.Garment-District.com.

Owner: Chris Cassel and Brooke Fletcher
Return Policy: Case by case basis
Try-on Facilities: Twenty private dressing rooms

The Garment District Inc. is a 16,000-square-foot transportation-themed (planes, subways, and cars) warehouse. Owners Cassel and Fletcher claim that they are the biggest vintage store in the region if not the country. "As a result, we don't specialize as much as try to cover every decade from the '40s until today, though we do have some pieces from before the '40s. We are probably strongest in '70s and '80s clothing, costumes, and Halloween, but our selection of '50s and before is still quite large. We also have a very popular dollar-a-pound section where we sell used clothing at 50 cents to $1.50 per pound."

Their favorite ears and styles? The '70s. "Though polyester has come and gone and come back again, it is still the most liberating style available. Mix and match at will. Bell-bottoms and flair pants just can't be beat."

"Fashion today is an amalgam of the past."
—JULIE WEISS, COSTUME DESIGNER FOR
AMERICAN BEAUTY AND *STEEL MAGNOLIAS*

Oona's Experienced Clothing

$

1210 Massachusetts Ave., Cambridge 02138; (617) 491-2654.
Open Mon–Sat: 11 a.m.–7 p.m., Sun: noon–6 p.m.

Owner: Kathleen White
Return Policy: All sales final
Try-on Facilities: Two private dressing rooms

Oona's Experienced Clothing, an "overindulgence of vintage clothing," has been located at Harvard Square for over 28 years. Every inch of this intimate four-room courtyard shop is jam packed with vintage goodies. Oona's has also done fundraising for local charities, including a 15-year-anniversary benefit for Rosie's Place, a shelter for battered women, and a 20-year-anniversary benefit for Cambridge Cares about Aids. "We are currently planning our 30-year-anniversary benefit for 2002," says White.

This shop specializes in affordable clothing and accessories for the vintage enthusiast as well as costumes for theme parties and decade dances. "Fashion repeats itself, and by recycling clothing, we offer a product both unusual and authentic. We carry fashions from the '20s through the '70s and beyond, with '80s fashions now becoming more popular," says White. Customers tend to favor fashions of the '60s and '70s for partywear and '20s flapper dresses as formalwear.

"In the 28 years we've been open," adds White, "we've sold clothes to celebrities John Lennon, Yoko Ono, Joe Penny, PJ Harvey, Jonathan Richman, Tony Perkins, Berry Berenson, Norman Mailer, Non's Church, Elizabeth Taylor, and members of Aerosmith, the Cars, the B-52's, the Cramps, Sonic Youth, BR-549, Pearl Jam, the Bosstones, and the Outlaws."

Additional Vintage Stores

Closet Upstairs: 223 Newbury St., Boston 02116; (617) 267-5757.

Great Eastern Trading Company: 49 River St., Cambridge 02139; (617) 354-5279.

DESIGNER RESALE BOUTIQUE

$$

419 Worcester Rd., Framingham 01701; (508) 626-0900.
Open Tues–Sat: 11 a.m.–4:30 p.m.

Owner: Harriet Canepari
Return Policy: All sales final
Try-on Facilities: Private dressing rooms

Designer Resale Boutique is both a "high-end designer resale store and funky boutique that doesn't want to compete with the nearby mall or discount stores. People shop here for unique coats, dresses, bags, and jewelry," says Canepari. Fur coats, novelty socks, and Bruno Magli shoes abound. Designers include Escada, Armani, Ralph Lauren, DKNY, Joseph Abboud, St. John, Anne Klein, Eileen Fisher, Dana Buchman, Calvin Klein, and Ellen Tracy. Canepari's personal collection includes an artsy black leather purse set in a Bakelite frame and a huge four ply shawl—pure luxury. This shop specializes in current fashion including cashmere and natural fibers and unknown hip designers for every age. "Set your own trend, wear what you look good in—wear color," says Canepari.

Current offerings include last year's leather Chanel and Escada purses, St. John's Knits, Ani Barrie sweaters, Max & Mabel vests, and Armani suits and jackets.

DRESS REHEARSAL

$$

252 Newbury St., Boston 02116; (617) 266-1113.
Open Mon–Sat: 11 a.m.–7 p.m., Sun: noon–6 p.m.

Owner: Deanna Sachez and Ted Sanchez
Return Policy: Exchange or store credit within seven days
Try-on Facilities: Two large fitting rooms

The foot became a focal point of fashion as mass production and the development of affordable synthetic fabrics granted everyone access to beautiful shoes.

1920s: Shoe styles were influenced by crazes like the Charleston, a dance that demanded a securely fastened shoe with a low heel and closed toe. High-tongued, cutaway patterns, the crossover, and the T-strap were other popular elements, though a single-bar pump with a pointed toe and one tiny covered button was the most common style. Bright fabrics and brilliantly dyed leather, including metallics, were used to create some of the most exciting shoes ever seen. The heels were often works of art in themselves. Made of such materials as Bakelite (a pressed plastic made from heating phenol with formaldehyde), Wedgwood, jasperware, or leather, they were often decorated with lace, rhinestones, and other pretty, shiny things. Fabulous harem slippers and slides were among the favorites.

1930s: A sturdy or clubby look was popular in women's footwear; shoes had rounded toes and low, heavy heels. Also debuted was the sling-back shoe, a ladies dress shoe with high heel, often open-toed and open-backed with a strap at the heel. The wedge sandal was another new style with two- to three-inch platform soles combined with high heels. Heels for day and evening wear grew higher and more slender as the decade progressed. Platform shoes appeared in the late '30s created from wood, cork, and other materials due to the shortage of leather and the WW II ban on rubber. A precursor of things to come, somber colors such as maroon, black, brown, and navy were frequently used.

1940s: Every imaginable material was incorporated into shoes, but reptile skins and mesh were the most successful substitutes for leather. Cork or wood soled "Wedgies" were another staple. By necessity, trims and embellishments were kept to a minimum. Women everywhere used household items, including cellophane and pipe cleaners, to create festive shoe decorations. U.S. rationing rules limited the height of shoe heels to one inch and allowed for only six color choices.

1950s: Charles Jourdan introduced a new kind of shoe style, the stiletto heel, in 1951. As time went on the goal was for the slimmest possible heel, eliminating earlier "chunky" styles. The pump was the basic shoe, but its toes might be cut, the vamps curved or cut into enticing Vs, or the heels molded into a variety of shapes. Every color of the rainbow was used; shoes were intended to match an outfit perfectly. Saddle shoes, penny loafers, and colored sneakers were popular with teenaged bobbysoxers. Sandals, ballet slippers, and other casual footwear became fashionable as casual outdoor activities became popular. Sandals, ballet slippers, and other casual footwear became increasingly fashionable as pool parties and other casual outdoor activities became popular.

1960s: Shoes reflected a rampant experimentation with color, texture, shape, and style. From citrus-colored sandals to spacey, iridescent rainbow platforms to classic colonial—or Edwardian-style pumps, young people gobbled up all the boots, sandals, and shoes that designers could turn out. Vinyl and plastic shoes made their debut, and go-go boots were popularized by the Nancy Sinatra song, "These Boots Were Made for Walking." A white, flat-heeled version of the boot was first created by designer Andrés Courrèges, followed by other designers in a variety of colors, materials, and styles.

1970s: Designers pushed the envelope by decorating shoes for adoring and outrageous customers such as Elton John, David Bowie, and Cher. Platform shoes rose to new heights, 7- to 8-inch stacked heels covered in rhinestones and sequins. A more conservative approach included simple pumps, sandals, and boots. Nike debuted in 1972 and the athletic craze was off and running.

1980s: Flats and low-heeled shoes in muted colors and classic styles were popular. Moccasins, espadrilles, and other kinds of native shoes were reinvented using new color palettes. Jellies, made of molded plastic in a variety of colors, were a hot fad.

Dress Rehearsal offers Armani, Versace, Richard Tyler, Donna Karan, St. John's Knits, Calvin Klein, Krizia, and Ferragamo in a "Victorian meets '20s art deco atmosphere. I love everything unique and different," says Sanchez. "That's why we carry jewelry in styles of the '20s, '60s, '70s, and '80s. Clothing can't be boring, unless it's a black-tie dress or business suit." The most interesting piece the Sanchez's have personally collected is an original '50s Christian Dior silk flower hat. Although this shop carries contemporary resale, they love the '20s because of the creativity put into women's dresses, jewelry, makeup, and fur coats.

KEEZER'S CLASSIC CLOTHING SINCE 1895
$$

140 River St., Cambridge 02139; (617) 547-2455.
Open Mon–Sat: 10 a.m.–6 p.m.
www.keezers.com

Owner: Leonard Goldstein
Return Policy: Only if the tailor cannot fix
Try-on Facilities: Four dressing rooms with full-length mirrors

Keezer's Classic Clothing Since 1895 carries men's clothing from designers such as Armani, Ermenegildo Zegna, Marzotto, Oxxford, and Hickey-Freeman. "People in Cambridge tend to dress conservatively, so we carry all work-appropriate dark colors. There are many formal events at Harvard and MIT, so half of our business is new and used formalwear," says Goldstein. "This store is probably the oldest used clothing store in the United States. It was founded in 1895 by Max Keezer, whose parents came from Holland in the 1860s. At the turn of the century, Harvard was a gentleman's school. Many men sent their sons east for a 'gentleman's education.' They would give the local tailor money to hand-make clothing for their sons. These smart young men would wear their new suit for one or two seasons and then bring it in for some cash. John F. Kennedy used to send his valet in every spring with his cast off clothing to sell.

"I have owned this business for over 23 years. We stock old Raccoon coats; men's capes handmade in England; handmade suits from London; pure cashmere coats from Oxford; and Chesterfield overcoats made from Montagnac material from France; all of which I count among my favorites," says Goldstein. "I even have a suit that was made for Paul Sorvino," he adds, which he found when cleaning old wardrobe out of a New York warehouse.

Goldstein especially enjoys men's formal accessories from the teens, '20s, and '30s; men's tails from the '30s; pinstripe suits from the '40s; sharkskin suits from the late '50s and early '60s; and tuxedos from the mid-'60s with narrow shawl lapels.

Additional Resale Stores

Closet: 175 Newbury St., Boston 02116; (617) 536-1919.

Models Resale Consignment Shop: 969 Concord St., Framingham 01701; (508) 875-9094.

Resale Shop: 12 Hurd Rd., Belmont 02478; (617) 484-8080.

Second Appearance: 801 Washington St., Newton 02460; (617) 527-7655.

Second Time Around Collections: 167 Newbury St., Boston 02116; (617) 247-3504; or 8 Eliot St., Cambridge 02138; (617) 491-7185.

Turnabout Shoppe: 30 Grove St., Wellesley 02482; (781) 237-4450.

NEW YORK CITY

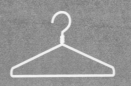

New York is one of the great cities of the world, known for its Broadway theater, famed museums and galleries, and as the center of the American fashion business (nicknamed by its usual location, "Seventh Avenue"). It is undeniably one of the great shopping centers of world!

High profile people in the arts, politics, theater, and business attend many opening nights, parties, award events, and charity balls, and cannot be seen and photographed more than once in their finery. No surprise then, that resale shops abound, full of recycled clothes from the rich and famous. A gown is worn once and off to the resale store it goes, where it lives until some lucky customer finds it for a fraction of the original price.

The availability of good vintage on the East Coast also reflects its location. When Los Angeles was barely in diapers, New York was already a huge metropolis, hence the abundance of clothing from the past still being dug out from grandmas' attics all over the more densely populated Eastern states.

New York was also the entrance for different ethnic groups that arrived in America in the early 1900s. Their European heritage lent a unique flavor to many neighborhoods where they first settled, and their contribution and character helped define the city and the country. Many immigrants worked in the sweat shops of early Seventh Avenue, but the sons and daughters of many became America's top fashion designers, creating clothes we love to collect, wear, and preserve today.

Though enormous in scope, New York is an easy city to navigate, the efficient—if not altogether beautiful—subway and the abundance of taxis. So put on comfy shoes and fill your purse with green stuff.

LET'S GO SHOPPING!

ANDY'S CHEE-PEES

$–$$$

691 Broadway, NYC 10012; (212) 420-5980.
Open Mon–Sat: 11 a.m.–9 p.m., Sun: 11 a.m.–8 p.m.
andyscheepees.citysearch.com

> *Owner:* Andy
> *Return Policy:* All sales final
> *Try-on Facilities:* Four dressing rooms upstairs, three downstairs

Andy's Chee-Pees offers Bill Blass, Bob Mackie, Lillian Couture, Pucci, Chapman, and Dior in a store that showcases vintage dresses, gabardine jackets, kimonos, and leather jackets along its walls. All stock is handpicked by Andy and includes equal amounts of men's and women's attire from the 1920s–70s, including leather, Army and Navy stuff, Dickies, vintage buttons and patches, hard rock '80s shirts, men's '70s leather coats, and men's '40s and '50s gabardine jackets, along with vintage belts, hats, gloves, and scarves. For women, look for beaded '20s dresses, turn-of-the-century bodices, real and fake furs, great beaded sweaters, hoop skirts and crinolines, '80s ruffled skirts, wedding dresses, and designer '40s and '60s couture dresses. Andy also has lots of great '70s pieces that are in good condition.

The most interesting piece Andy has collected was a silk and velvet riding coat with silk lace from the late 19th century. Naomi Campbell tried it on in her teens before she was famous. His favorite period is the '40s for the wonderful focus on detailing.

KELLY OSBOURNE attended the 2002 *Maxim* Hot 100 party in a vintage denim jacket (over a Helmut Lang top and a long black skirt).

ANNA

$–$$

150 E. Third St., NYC 10009; (212) 358-0195.
Open Mon–Fri: 1 p.m.–8 p.m., Sat/Sun: 1 p.m.–7 p.m.

Owner: Kathy Kemp
Return Policy: Within three days for store credit
Try-on Facilities: One dressing room

ANNA, a small boutique of minimal design, specializes in vintage pieces that work with current styles and unique pieces that inspire Kemp as a designer. She's been in business for six years and the stock changes weekly, but she always carries vintage lingerie. ANNA supplied wardrobe for *Almost Famous.*

The most interesting piece Kemp has collected would be "either a Pucci velvet skirt circa 1970 or a Vivienne Westwood couture gown, long, bias, of red silk." Her favorite period "changes with fashion. I guess I like them all, but regardless of era, I always seem to collect vintage lingerie. I live in New York City, so space is an issue. Most pieces are small, layerable, and more timeless than outerwear."

BEACON'S CLOSET

$

110 Bedford Ave., Brooklyn 11211; (718) 486-0816.
Open Mon–Fri: noon–9 p.m., Sat/Sun: 11 a.m.–8 p.m.
www.beaconscloset.com

Owner: Carrie Peterson and Sam Fogarino
Return Policy: Within seven days of purchase with tag attached and receipt
Try-on Facilities: Five dressing rooms with large mirrors

Beacon's Closet is "mod and pink and red and bitchin'", offering Prada, Gucci, Betsey Johnson, and Vivienne Westwood, among others. Founded in 1997, Peterson and Fogarino boast over 2000 square feet of vintage and ultra-modern secondhand clothing. They specialize in hipster styles, because "the store's location demands it." The most interesting piece they've collected? "Punky Brewsters' leather coat—or so we were told."

CHEAP JACK VINTAGE CLOTHING

$–$$$

841 Broadway, NYC 10003; (212) 995-0403.
Open Mon–Sat: 11 a.m.–8 p.m., Sun: noon–7 p.m.

> **Owner:** Jacob
> **Return Policy:** All sales final
> **Try-on Facilities:** Dressing room

Cheap Jack Vintage Clothing is three floors of an eclectic mix of 1920s–80s vintage dresses, men's pants, shirts, vintage T-shirts, Pucci, Armani, Dolce & Gabbana—everything! Jacob specializes in the '20s, because the majority of his clients want mint-condition '20s clothing. Jacob's favorite period, however, is the '70s because of the colorful, flashy styles and attention to detail. One of the most interesting pieces he has collected is one of the first pairs of Levi's ever made.

CHERRY

$$

185 Orchard St., NYC 10002; (212) 358-7131.
Open Daily: noon–7 p.m.

> **Owner:** Radford Brown and Cesar Padilla
> **Return Policy:** All sales final
> **Try-on Facilities:** One dressing room with two mirrors

Cherry caters to a very diverse clientele. "We focus on designer vintage, but good form and design are important. We also have a strong rock 'n' roll base and our range goes from punk rock to classic," say owners Brown and Padilla. They offer a large Kansai Yamamoto collection, along with Yves Saint Laurent, Cardin, Pucci, Gucci, Ossie Clark, Jean Muir, and Courrèges.

The most interesting pieces the owners have collected are '70s artwear pieces from the Julie store in NYC, Gernreich sample plastic dresses, and a '60s Sant'Angelo shawl dress. They love space age Cardin, Rabánne, Courrèges, and Gernreich.

Current offerings include: a '70s Courrèges orange vinyl full-length coat with logo; a '60s Pucci velvet handbag with abstract design; and a '70s Zandra Rhodes green chiffon feather design dress. You've seen clothing from this store on HBO's *Sex and the City.*

COBBLESTONES
$

314 E. Ninth St., NYC 10003; (212) 673-5372.
Open Tues–Sun: 1 p.m.–7 p.m.

> *Owner:* Delanee Coppersmith
> *Return Policy:* Case by case basis
> *Try-on Facilities:* Dressing room

Cobblestones, established in 1981, is a treasure trove that specializes in unique and unusual accessories, including handbags, hats, silk scarves, wallets, shoes, eyeglass cases, key cases, wide and skinny ties, summer sun hats, and lingerie. The most interesting piece Coppersmith has collected is a clear Lucite cigarette case. Her favorite periods are the '30s and '70s because of the cut of the clothing and rounded-toe shoes.

 wore a vintage blue velvet blazer (and Armani shirt) over classic Levi's to *Movieline's* 2002 Young Hollywood Awards.

DAVID OWENS VINTAGE CLOTHING

$$

154 Orchard St., NYC 10002; (212) 677-3301.
Open Tues–Sun: 11 a.m.–7 p.m.

> **Owner:** David Owens and Linda Lavalle
> **Return Policy:** Case by case basis
> **Try-on Facilities:** A dressing room constructed of vintage fabric

David Owens Vintage Clothing offers ties, fringe scarves, dresses, leathers, suede, and furs, but specializes in rayon and cotton Hawaiian shirts. He also carries a very large collection of men's accessories: peek-a-boo ties; hand-painted, silk-screened, and color photo ties; designer ties from the '40s and '50s; and a large collection of rayon fringe scarves. "We also specialize in outerwear for fall in wool, unusual antique leather, fur, and faux fur from the 1950s–80s."

Owens began selling vintage apparel in NYC in 1974, soon after migrating from the West Coast. Raised in Southern California, he grew up with a love of the ocean. As Owens developed his surfing and bodysurfing skills, it was only inevitable he would travel to the islands of Hawaii, where he developed a passion for Hawaiian shirts. He now stocks his store with a collection of cotton, rayon, and polyester Hawaiians. Styles run from the 1940s–70s in a wide selection of patterns, including women's blouses. There are always at least a dozen shirts of collectible quality available here.

Owens' private Hawaiian shirt collection is extensive—at least one hundred—some he won't show to anyone (except his wife), and they are kept in secret storage. His favorite label is the famous Duke Champion Kahanamoku: An Hawaiian Original. The best part of this story is that Owens wears these shirts—and "with class and style!" Even when he is hard at work in his vintage clothing business, he sports a cotton Hawaiian, usually from the '50s. He only wears his collectible, quality Hawaiians in the evening with casual pants.

Eye Candy

$$

329 Lafayette St., NYC 10012; (212) 343-4275.
Open Daily: noon–8 p.m.

> **Owner:** Ron Caldwell
> **Return Policy:** Exchange within 30 days
> **Try-on Facilities:** Dressing room with multiple mirrors

Eye Candy is a small store crammed full of exciting vintage accessories from Chanel, Dior, and other major labels gathered from Caldwell's travels all over the world. In business for over three years, Caldwell offers vintage and contemporary designer resale including lots of purses: everything from leather, Bakelite, straw, raffia, crocheted, and beaded to Enid Collins pictorial appliques on linen and wood (collectibles), and some original Whiting Davis mesh purses from the '20s. The most interesting piece Caldwell has ever collected is a Lucite-encrusted handbag with rhinestones, the size of a fishbowl. His favorite period is the 1940s–50s.

He carries jewelry and watches from all periods (Caldwell is a jewelry designer, so his eye is flawless), including antique designer and Dior jewelry. Also, look for shoes, fur jackets, and hats—winter hats, '50s men's straw hats (now popular with women), and Schiaparelli hats.

Caldwell feels there is something wonderful to be found in every period: Victorian jet mourning jewelry; '20s deco micro-beaded purses; '30s open-toe platform shoes with matching handbags; '40s Bakelite jewelry; '50s everything; '60s Pucci; '70s platform shoes; and '80s stilettos.

 HILARY SWANK sported a Randolph Duke gown accessorized with a Victorian-era diamond necklace when she accepted her Oscar for Best Actress at the 2000 Academy Awards.

THE FAMILY JEWELS
VINTAGE CLOTHING

$$–$$$

130 W. 23rd St., NYC 10011; (212) 633-6020.
Open Sun–Wed: 11 a.m.–7 p.m., Thurs–Sat: 11 a.m.–8 p.m.
www.FamilyJewelsNYC.com

Owner: Lillyan Peditto
Return Policy: All sales final
Try-on Facilities: Dressing room

The Family Jewels Vintage Clothing offers the best of American vintage from the Victorian period through the '70s for men and women, including designer pieces and fabulous nondesigner goods from all over the United States. They carry '30s silk nightgowns, '40s flowery rayon dresses, bridal gowns, sexy lingerie, men's and women's suits, beaded bags, vintage jewelry, hats, gloves, Lucite purses, leathers, and beautiful gowns and day dresses from Pucci, Bill Blass, Hattie Carnegie, and Oscar de la Renta.

The most interesting piece Peditto has collected is a '20s opera cape from Paris, with cut velvet and metallic threads and incredible textile patterns and colors. Her favorite periods are the '30s, '40s, and '50s for their "superior fabrics, fantastic construction (bias cuts), amazing textile patterns, sexy draped designs, '50s cinched waists, big crinoline skirts, and sexy capri pants."

The Family Jewels was named "one of the best vintage stores in the United States" by *Vogue, InStyle,* and *Elle* magazines and is frequently featured in fashion layouts in major magazines such as *W, Details,* Italian and American *Vogue, Vanity Fair, Elle,* and *Seventeen.* "International design houses such as Dolce & Gabbana, Giorgio Armani, Calvin Klein, Ralph Lauren, Jean Paul Gaultier, Andrea Pfister, Kenneth Cole, Adrienne Vittadini, Michael Kors, and Cynthia Rowley shop in our store for inspiration for today's fashions," says Peditto. "We are a one-stop shop for costume designers (of Woody Allen and Spike Lee films to name a few), wardrobe supervisors, photographers, and a favorite of fashion stylists who have put our clothing on celebrities such as Uma Thurman, Ethan Hawke, Twiggy, Cindy Crawford,

Courtney Love, David Bowie, Rosie O'Donnell, Johnny Depp, Debbie Mazar, Julia Roberts, and Diana Ross."

"If you look good and dress well, you don't need a

purpose in life."

—ROBERT PANTE, FASHION CONSULTANT

SIDE TRIP: WASHINGTON D.C.

VINTAGE

Bird-In-The-Cage Antiques: 110 King St., Alexandria, VA 22314; (703) 549-5114.

Meeps & Aunt Neensies Vintage: 1520 U St. Northwest, Washington D.C. 20009; (202) 265-6546.

DESIGNER RESALE

Encore Resale Dress Shop: 3715 Macomb St. Northwest, #201, Washington D.C. 20016; (202) 966-8122.

Secondhand Rose: 1516 Wisconsin Ave. Northwest, Washington D.C. 20007; (202) 337-3378.

Secondi: 1611 Connecticut Ave. Northwest, Floor 2, Washington D.C. 20009; (202) 667-1122.

Second Chance: 7702 Woodmont Ave., #205, Bethesda, MD 20814; (301) 652-6606.

MARMALADE

$–$$$

172 Ludlow St., NYC 10002; (212) 473-8070.
Open Daily: 12:30 p.m.–8:30 p.m.

Owner: Hannah Kurland
Return Policy: Store credit within ten days
Try-on Facilities: One dressing room with full-length mirror

Marmalade is a cozy, loungy store with clothing by designers Gloria Vanderbilt, Yves Saint Laurent, Norma Kamali, and Adolfo, arranged by color. Women's shoes are on a rack hanging from the ceiling, and the walls are painted in bright blocks of color. Kurland specializes in shoes and "fashion-current vintage." Her most interesting collectables are a "Rhodes" peach jacket and a pink leather quilted disco bag with three sacks hanging from one string.

Current offerings include black patent leather shoes from the '80s decorated with a white appliqué of the NY skyline.

MARY EFRON FINE AND RARE WEARABLES

$$–$$$

72 Thompson St, NYC 10012; (212) 219-3099.
Open Tues–Sun: 1 p.m.–7 p.m. and by appointment

Owner: Mary Efron
Return Policy: Case by case basis
Try-on Facilities: Dressing room

Mary Efron Fine and Rare Wearables currently has a fabulous silver 1920s beaded dress and a variety of '20s purses displayed in the window. Efron has been at this location for seven years but collected Dior, Norell, Vera Maxwell, and Claire McCardell for at least ten years before that. Her taste, she says, is eclectic, but she is especially appreciative of hand stitching. She likes witty clothes with "that special magic," eccentric evening bags, and exotic day bags. The most interesting piece she has collected is an 1895 skating jacket, though her favorite period is the era between WW I and WW II.

Mary Efron Fine and Rare Wearables is a very small store, but clothes are as "curatorially arranged as possible," says Efron. This shop offers clothing and accessories for women including: 1920s beaded bags and dresses; evening dresses from the '20s to the present; beaded cashmere sweaters; rayon printed pajamas from the '40s; Victorian shawls (one piano shawl circa 1850); and lingerie from the 1930s–50s. There is a huge variety of clothing; most are one-of-a-kind items and all are in excellent condition.

METROPOLIS

$

43 Third Ave., NYC 10003; (212) 358-0795.
Open Daily: noon–10 p.m.

Owner: Richard Colligan
Return Policy: Exchange only
Try-on Facilities: Three dressing rooms

Metropolis specializes in T-shirts and '80s wear. The most interesting piece Colligan has ever collected is a "pair of Winona Ryder's underwear." His favorite period is the '80s, because "that's when I first started to get laid," said Colligan.

"In times of economic uncertainty,
                    fashion always turns to Chanel."
                              —BILL BLASS

O MISTRESS MINE

$$–$$$

143 Seventh Ave. South, NYC 10014; (212) 691-4327.
Open Mon–Sat: 1 p.m.–7:30 p.m., Sun: 2 p.m.–6 p.m.
www.omistressmine.com

> **Owner:** Wanda Hanlon
> **Return Policy:** Store credit only
> **Try-on Facilities:** Dressing rooms with mirrors

O Mistress Mine has been in business for 33 years, offering classic ladies clothing and kimonos by designers such as Dior, Stone Martin, and Pauline Trigère, and a limited offering of men's smoking jackets. Hanlon's favorite period is the '30s, "because I like the way the skirts were put together." Her favorite look coordinates shoes with a handbag and hat. The most interesting pieces she has collected are museum-quality Victorian items such as beaded Victorian jackets and Edwardian dresses.

Current offerings include: a sweet little polished cotton black '50s sundress with spaghetti straps and tiny pink flowers and matching wrap; a '40s black crepe dress with silver and blue beads on the sleeves running all the way up the collar; and a '40s full-length Stone Martin coat.

THE 1909 COMPANY + CHELSEA-GIRL.COM

$$

63 Thompson St., NYC 10012; (212) 343-1658.
Open Daily: noon–7 p.m.
www.Chelsea-Girl.com

> **Owner:** Elisa Casas
> **Return Policy:** Store sales final
> **Try-on Facilities:** Dressing room

The 1909 Company + Chelsea-Girl.com is an inviting boutique, with bay windows and a tin ceiling, in an old building that stocks Pucci, Gucci, Hermès, Valentino, Missoni, Hattie Carnegie, Ceil Chapman, Claire McCardell, Diana von Furstenberg, North Beach Leather, Adele Simpson, Oscar de la Renta, Bill Blass, Geofrey Beene, Lilly Pulitzer, Mollie Parnis, Givenchy, and Bonnie Cashin.

"We specialize in wearable (versus collectible) vintage clothing and accessories," says Casas. "Many of our pieces are by well-known designers, but labels are not what we look for. We look for unusual detailing, beautiful fabrics, and, above all, styles that work with a modern wardrobe. Our passion is purses—whimsical or practical, but always beautiful. We have the best selection of vintage purses in New York."

Casas' favorite find? "Asking a vintage fanatic to choose their favorite pieces is like asking a mother to choose her favorite child! But here goes: a rare Schiaparelli purse that lights up; a French '30s purse shaped like a lute; a hand-painted Ceil Chapman chiffon gown; and my "holey" cashmere cardigan." Casas' favorite period is the '30s because the clothing is very easy to wear and the lines (long and lean) are modern and easily mixed with new pieces. "We especially love '30s knitwear and evening wear." You've seen their wares on *Titanic* and *Sex and the City*.

Physical Graffiti

$$

96 St. Marks Pl., NYC 10009; (212) 477-7334
Open Sun–Wed: 1 p.m.–9 p.m., Thurs–Sat: 1 p.m.–10 p.m.

Owner: Ilana Malka
Return Policy: All sales final
Try-on Facilities: Dressing rooms with mirrors

Physical Graffiti is a cozy shop in which Malka offers handpicked Pucci, Wayne Roberts, Vera, Gucci, and Prada. She specializes in the 1970s–80s, because "that is what's most in demand right now." The most interesting piece Malka collected is a '40s silk hand-painted Chinese robe, and her favorite period is the 1940s–60s "because of the interesting cuts."

Current stock includes a '30s sheer, crocheted black gown and go-go dresses.

RAGS-A-GOGO

$

218 W. 14th St., NYC 10011; (646) 486-4011
Open Daily: noon–8 p.m.
www.RagsAGoGo.com

Owner: Natalie Fuz and Suzanne Ethier
Return Policy: Exchange only within two weeks
Try-on Facilities: Dressing rooms

Rags-a-gogo specializes in secondhand street fashion, because "the fashion industry gets its ideas mainly from retro and vintage items. If we present the authentic at great prices, it sells!" say Fuz and Ethier. They have no favorite period, because "all periods are fun to mix and match and play with, from the '40s until now." Favorite collectables include: a pair of miner's 1928 Levi's; a WW II flight jacket; and a 1940s two-pocket "Big E" Levi's jacket. Celebrities who have shopped at this store include Julia Roberts, Courtney Love, and David Bowie. Their garments have been used for TV shows and commercials, photos, and music video and magazine shoots for Lauryn Hill, Mariah Carey, and Drew Barrymore to name a few.

 KIRSTEN DUNST wore vintage Emmanuel Ungaro to the 2002 Hollywood opening of *Spider Man*.

REMINISCENCE

$

50 W. 23rd St., NYC 10010; (212) 243-2292.
Open Mon–Sat: 11 a.m.–7:30 p.m., Sun: noon–7 p.m.
www.reminiscence.com

> *Owner:* Stewart Richer
> *Return Policy:* All vintage sales final
> *Try-on Facilities:* Six dressing rooms with full-length mirrors

Reminiscence offers mostly '60s and '70s clothing with some '40s and '50s items. The store is decorated with '40s and '50s furniture with a '50s bar for a display counter, and eclectic vintage mannequins dotted around. Richer's favorite collectable? "A '50s circle skirt, all hand done, embroidered with Disney characters."

Current offerings include: Western fringed jackets from the '70s; French tank tops made of lace; and ladies '60s coats with big collars.

SIDE TRIP: PHILADELPHIA

VINTAGE

Ballyhoo: 213 New St., Philadelphia 19106; (215) 627-1700.

Pennyfeathers: 1312 South St., Philadelphia 19147; (215) 772-1945.

Vintage Clothing Co.: 530 S. Fourth St., Philadelphia 19147; (215) 925-7607.

DESIGNER RESALE

Buffalo Exchange Ltd.: 1109 Walnut St., Philadelphia 19107; (215) 627-4647.

RESURRECTION
$$$

217 Mott St., NYC 10012; (212) 625-1374.
Open Mon–Sat: 11 a.m.–7 p.m., Sun: noon–5 p.m.

Owner: Varies
Return Policy: Case by case basis
Try-on Facilities: Dressing rooms

Resurrection has avant-garde '60s, rockin' '70s, and fun '80s items with a swipe of chic—clothing for rock 'n' rollers, unique party hosts and hostesses, and outerwear. The décor of the NYC store is very different from the minimalist Resurrection on Melrose Avenue in Los Angeles (see p. 65). Designers featured seemed to be from the '70s and '80s; spotted on a recent visit was a Holly Harp dress from the '80s. You've seen their clothes in *Charlie's Angels,* Jennifer Lopez videos, *Ally McBeal, That '70s Show, Dharma & Greg,* and *Sex and the City.*

....

SEARCH AND DESTROY
$–$$

25 St. Marks Pl., NYC 10003; (212) 358-1120.
Open Mon–Thurs: 1 p.m.–10 p.m., Fri/Sat: 1 p.m.–1 a.m.,
Sun: 1 p.m.–midnight.

Owner: Yuji Umeki
Return Policy: All sales final
Try-on Facilities: Two dressing rooms with mirrors

Search and Destroy carries clothing from the '40s to '80s, including great leather, fun Japanese-print coats, sneakers, handbags, Western boots and shirts, men's pants, T-shirts, coats, and fur coats. This trendy store showcases its fun items on the walls. Umeki specializes in the '70s and '80s because that is what's popular, offering lots of denim jackets and fur coats for the ladies.

SOUTHPAW VINTAGE CLOTHING & TEXTILES

$$$

226 W. 37th St., 8th Floor, NYC 10018; (212) 244-2768.
Open Mon–Fri: 9:30 a.m.–6:30 p.m. by appointment only.

Owner: Jeffrey Pattie and Nick Michael
Return Policy: Exchange within two days
Try-on Facilities: Multiple changing rooms with mirrors

Southpaw Vintage Clothing & Textiles is a complete design resource for men's and women's vintage apparel, accessories, and textiles, for rent or purchase Pattie and Michael's a " '70s drug lord meets Al Green boudoir" studio. Designers carried include biba, Janice Wainwright, Halston, Jean Muir, Bill Gibb, Thierry Mugler, Claude Montana, Yuki, Sonia Rykiel, Scott Barrie, Chloé, Vivienne Westwood, Complice, Jean-Louis Scherrer, Stephen Sprouse, and Rudi Gernreich. "We have the best Stephen Burrows collection in the world," says Michael. "Handmade '30s chiffon gowns that are works of art."

Pattie and Michael travel the world constantly to select the most unique pieces from many periods in time. Their library includes vintage couture as well as one-of-a-kind, handmade items, and an extensive collection of knitwear, lingerie, and hand-beaded and embroidered garments. "We have clients from every aspect of the fashion industry who shop for haute couture collections through '70s moderne; we are a vintage department store," says Michael. "Thankfully more and more people are learning to appreciate fine vintage clothing and textiles due to films, television, and the celebrities who wear vintage so stunningly."

The owner's favorite period is the '70s, because "it was a great time for experimentation and originality in both men and women's clothing. There were so many fabulous themes, many of which had a distinct sexiness to them, and many of which are still, and always will be, relevant."

Current offerings include: a lizard skin Ossie Clark trench coat made for Jimi Hendrix's last girlfriend; a Stephen Burrows suede and jersey multi-colored wrap jacket and culottes; and an emerald green and gold lamé bias cut '30s dress previously owned by Wallis Simpson.

STAR STRUCK, LTD.

$–$$

47 Greenwich Ave., NYC 10014; (212) 691-5357.
Open Mon–Sat: 11 a.m.–8 p.m., Sun: noon–7 p.m.

> **Owner:** Joseph and Michele Markus
> **Return Policy:** Exchange or credit only
> **Try-on Facilities:** Three dressing rooms

STAR STRUCK, LTD., organized by style and size, specializes in men's and women's clothing from the 1930s–60s, with some '70s. "We carry only the best of the best, including Hawaiian shirts, Western shirts, and grade 'A' used Levi's." Says Markus, "Much of our merchandise is new-old, in perfect condition. Our prices are more than fair, and we take pride in our merchandise." The most interesting piece that the Markus' have collected is a Civil War coat, "purchased from us by a museum." Their favorite period is the '40s for "the style, quality, and detail." Clothing from this store has been used in *Carlito's Way, Donnie Brasco, The Cowboy Way* with Woody Harrelson, *Goodfellas, Saturday Night Live, Sex and the City,* and *The Sopranos.*

THE STELLA DALLAS LOOK

$–$$

218 Thompson St., NYC 10012; (212) 674-0447.
Open Daily noon–7 p.m.

> **Owner:** Carol Atkin
> **Return Policy:** All sales final
> **Try-on Facilities:** Two roomy dressing rooms

The Stella Dallas Look, in business for 25 years (10 years at this location), gathers 1940s–60s merchandise from estate sales and dealers. This warm and comfortable boutique-sized store is decorated with vintage mannequins and specializes in the '40s and '50s, "the age of elegance, fine workmanship, and beautiful materials." Look for fitted jackets and tailored coats from the '40s, honeymoon lingerie from Jean Harlow's era, and Cabana Club luncheon and party dresses from the '50s. They also carry leather for men and women, vintage ties, jewelry, and purses. "We are a famous resource for silk scarves, shawls, and men's tuxedo mufflers. And we make evening purses, fur hats, and embroidered sweaters out of vintage materials."

Interesting pieces in Atkins' collection include "an exquisite white silk and satin three-piece Victorian ensemble with a note attached that read, 'My aunt Anna made this for her graduation from high school,' and a turn-of-the-century dress from a dealer in New Orleans. While examining it, I found a small square pocket inside the left sleeve seam that was made of the same fabric as the dress. Inside the hidden pocket, I found a dollar bill dated 1899, with Lincoln and Grant pictured."

Atkins' favorite period? "The '40s, when women stepped forward and ran the home front for a nation at war. Their man-tailored suits, shoulder pads, and jaunty fedoras expressed confidence and competency. Yet the corset fit of the jackets and the silk and lace lingerie revealed uncompromised femininity."

Current offerings include: '40s print dresses; '50s cotton dresses, always popular for summer; and a variety of cotton skirts, hankies, and scarves. Their bathing suits are also popular items. Atkins also offers customers a "Sewer's Hotline" newsletter with tips for repair, restoration, and care of vintage clothes.

"A designer is only as good as the star who
wears her clothes."

—EDITH HEAD

SWIMWEAR FROM RESERVED TO REVEALING

The first recorded use of bathing apparel comes from Greece around 300 BC. Yet the 20th century saw more changes in one hundred years than the previous two thousand! And here is how it all happened.

1900: Ladies wore bathing costumes, essentially black, knee-length wool dresses with long stockings and lace-up footwear. This modest and impractical outfit was completed with a hat or bathing bonnet.

1910s: Bathing dresses shortened slightly, stockings sometimes disappeared, and necklines dipped a bit.

1920s: Formfitting wool tank suits with built-in undershorts were the most common swimwear seen. They stopped mid-thigh and came only in black or primary colors, often sporting stripes or modern art-style abstracts. Bathing caps completed the look.

1930s: Itchy wool was replaced with gaily printed cottons as swimwear took on a new formfitting, feminine look. Undershorts finally disappeared, leaving a modesty panel across the front. Midriffs were bared, first through cutouts in tank suits, then with the emergence of the two-piece suit.

1940s: Esther Williams set trends, and Dorothy Lamour's sarong was seen on women all over. Lingerie companies ventured into the swimwear market, introducing one-piece suits resembling corsets (often just as uncomfortable) with built-in bras, zippers, elastic, and boning.

1946: The bikini debuted in Paris, but American shores shunned the tiny two-piece until around 1960.

1960s: The bikini was popularized in Frankie Avalon and Annette Funicello movies, such as *How to Stuff a Wild Bikini*, although puritanical Annette rarely actually wears a bikini in any of her films. Swimsuit designer Rudi Gernreich unveiled the topless swimsuit.

1970s: Fabrics improved, and Lycra became the universal preference. Soft-constructed maillots became common—the two-piece maillot was a great alternative for those not daring enough to sport a bikini. Bikinis shrank, and in 1977 the Brazilian tanga, or thong, hit the beaches.

1980s: The French-cut swimsuit raised leg openings high on the hips, and thong bikinis became common among the young.

TOKYO JOE, INC.

$$–$$$

334 E. 11th St., NYC 10003; (212) 473-0724.
Open Daily noon–9 p.m.

> **Owner:** Joe Handa
> **Return Policy:** Case by case basis
> **Try-on Facilities:** One dressing room with mirrors

Tokyo Joe, Inc. carries Issey Miyake, Comme des Garçons, Marc Jacobs sweaters, vintage Pucci, and Dior and Chanel gowns and jackets from 1960s–80s.

Also at 240 E. 28th St., NYC 10016; (212) 532-3605.

WHAT COMES AROUND GOES AROUND

$–$$$

351 W. Broadway, NYC 10013; (212) 343-9303.
Open Mon–Sat: 11 a.m.–8 p.m., Sun: noon–7 p.m.
www.nyvintage.com

> **Owner:** Seth Weisser, Gerard Maione, and Robert Melet
> **Return Policy:** Store credit within seven days
> **Try-on Facilities:** Three dressing rooms

What Comes Around Goes Around is housed in a beautiful building that was erected in the 1880s. Designed to resemble a 19th-century dry goods store, Weisser, Maione, and Melet restored their space using woods and fixtures from that period. They have men's and women's clothing and accessories from the 1880s–1980s by Gucci, Dior, Pucci, Courrèges, Ossie Clark and almost everyone else. Weisser, Maione, and Melet travel the world searching for specialty vintage pieces.

This shop has "the country's largest collection of vintage denim, an extensive collection of 1960s–80s designer woman's clothing and accessories, and a huge Hawaiian, Western, and gabardine stock. We also feature a strong military and workwear collection. In women's, we have period dresses from the 1930s–70s and much more. Our collection includes more than 60,000 garments."

They sold a pair of original 1890s Levi's jeans to a museum, and they currently have three Dior dresses from the estate of the Duchess of Windsor. Their favorite period is the '60s because of the diversity of the clothing modernists like Courrèges and Pierre Cardin and the beginning of the hippie movement with great leather and suede.

Additional Vintage Stores

Alice Underground: 481 Broadway, NYC 10013; (212) 431-9067.

Foley & Corinna: 108 Stanton St., NYC 10002; (212) 529-2338.

Jim Smiley Vintage Clothing: 128 W. 23rd St., NYC 10011; (212) 741-1195.

Tokio 7: 64 E. 7th St., NYC 10003; (212) 353-8443.

"Style is primarily a matter of instinct."
—BILL BLASS

BIS DESIGNER RESALE

$$–$$$

1134 Madison Avenue, NYC 10028; (212) 396-2760.
Open Mon–Fri: 10 a.m.–7 p.m., Sat: 10 a.m.–6 p.m., Sun: noon–5 p.m.
www.bisbiz.com

Owner: Odiana and Henri Dauman
Return Policy: All sales final
Try-on Facilities: Private dressing rooms

BIS DESIGNER RESALE is an elegant, upscale, well-lit boutique with a dark wood display case of purses and jewelry. Offering 50 to 75 percent off new retail, the Dauman's carry both vintage and contemporary resale items from high-end American and European designers such as Prada, Hermès, Valentino, and Chanel at amazing prices. Their vintage fashions, which are tastefully altered to reflect the latest trends, include Emilio Pucci, Pauline Trigère, Bonnie Cashin, and Roberta di Camerino.

They also carry Adrienne Vittadini, Alaïa, Anne Klein, Armani, Balenciaga, Bally, Byblos, Bill Blass, Bottega Veneta, Burberry, Calvin Klein, Céline, Cerruti, Chlöe, Christan Louboutin, Christian Dior, Christian Lacroix, Claude Montana, Coach, Dana Buchman, Dolce & Gabbana, Donna Karan, Dries Van Noten, Emanuel Ungaro, Escada, Evan-Picone, Fendi, Geoffrey Beene, Gianfranco Ferre, Givenchy, Gucci, Guy Laroche, Halston, Helmut Lang, Isaac Mizrahi, Jean-Paul Gaultier, Jil Sander, John Galliano, Judith Lieber, Karl Lagerfeld, Kate Spade, Kenzo, Kors, Leonard, Levi's, Loro Piana, Louis Vuitton, Manolo Blahnik, Marc Jacobs, Mary McFadden, Max Mara, Missoni, Mondi, Moschino, Nicole Miller, Oscar de la Renta, Paloma Picasso, Ralph Lauren, Rena Lange, Richard Tyler, Salvatore Ferragamo, Sonia Rykiel, St. John, Stephane Kelian, Thierry Mugler, Vera Wang, Versace, Yohji Yamamoto, and Yves Saint Laurent.

The most interesting pieces the Daumans have collected include a Bonnie Cashin hooded storm coat from the '60s, and handmade haute couture garments by Yves Saint Laurent and Coco Chanel. Their favorite period is the '60s and '70s fashion explosion, and they love NYC, "because it is and was the fashion capitol of the world when American designers Calvin Klein, Bill Blass, Anne Klein, and Ralph Lauren began climbing the ladder to international fame."

LA BOUTIQUE RESALE

$–$$$

1045 Madison Ave., 2nd Floor, NYC 10021; (212) 517-8099.
Open Mon–Sat: 11 a.m.–7 p.m., Sun: noon–6 p.m.
www.LaBoutiqueResale.com

> **Owner:** Jonathan Tse
> **Return Policy:** All sales final
> **Try-on Facilities:** Four dressing rooms

La Boutique Resale is a spacious, elegant store offering a wide selection of upscale designer Chanel, Gucci, St. John, Prada, Armani, and Issey Miyake clothing and accessories, vintage Pucci, Halston, Gucci, Courrèges, Pauline Trigère, Alaïa, and 1960s–80s collectible fashion. The most interesting piece that Tse has collected is an early '60s black Schiaparelli gown and matching mink-trimmed cape. His favorite period is the '70s, "a period that had no distinct reproduced style. It was a period when designers and their fans were free to express themselves from one extreme to the other, whether sexy, hippie, or conservative."

The racks here are loaded with blue-chip designers, so it isn't hard to find a little black Dolce & Gabbana dress, a scarlet Hervé Léger gown, or tons of Chanel jewelry. Shoes by Missoni, Dolce & Gabbana, Yves Saint Laurent, and Ralph Lauren are in excellent condition or unworn.

 used vintage art deco cufflinks on his Ozwald Boateng suit at the 2002 Academy Awards.

BROOKLYN SUGAR

$$

322 Fifth Ave., Park Slope, Brooklyn 11215; (718) 369-3295.
Hours are seasonal, call for current hours.
www.brooklynsugarshop.com

Owner: Micole Taggart
Return Policy: Case by case basis
Try-on Facilities: One huge fitting room that customers occasionally share

Brooklyn Sugar, the creation of Brooklyn-born Taggart, is named after—herself! Her husband calls her Sugar, and the nickname fit her store perfectly. Vintage clothing has always been a part of her life, even as a little girl. "My mother loved and appreciated handcrafts such as embroidery and really fine details on clothing," says Taggart. "I, in turn, especially love the '40s because of the handwork and attention to detail."

Previously a 40-year-old hardware store, Brooklyn Sugar is 650 square feet of contemporary resale and vintage, along with collections by young, up-and-coming designers. This store has maintained its original subway tile floor, turquoise tin ceiling adorned with bright fake flowers, a "dressing room fit for a king or queen," and walls decorated with the work of local artists. Taggart loves '50s inspired prints and kitsch pieces from the '80s. Vintage labels offered include Pucci, Gucci, Yves Saint Laurent, and Vera Wang. Contemporary labels include Betsey Johnson, Diane von Furstenberg, and Lilly Pulitzer.

DESIGNER RESALE CORP.

$–$$$

324 E. 81st St., NYC 10028; (212) 734-3639.
Open Mon–Fri: 11 a.m.–7 p.m., Sat: 10 a.m.–6 p.m., Sun: noon–5 p.m.

Owner: Mylna Skoller
Return Policy: All sales final
Try-on Facilities: Five dressing rooms

Designer Resale Corp. offers current styles by Chanel, Hermès, Prada, Armani, and other well-known designers. The owner carefully selects and personally prices all items to maintain the international reputation of this store, which has been featured in magazines worldwide.

Opened 11 years ago in the basement of one brownstone, it now has expanded to adjacent basement rooms across four buildings. It's very cozy and fun to explore, with carpeted floors and exposed brick walls. Merchandise largely consists of suits and business attire, with a limited stock of eveningwear, and lots of purses, hats, and shoes. Currently there is a cream colored beaded Carmen Marc Valvo evening gown and a Dooney & Bourke unused tote bag, among other offerings.

Twice a year the store has a huge sale; people line up outside waiting to get in. Savings are 30 to 50 percent, and on the last day items are 80 percent off. The remaining clothes are donated to charity, and new merchandise is brought up from the basement. Skoller is discreet about her consignors but hints that celebrities and Washington senators are among her clients.

Next door from Designer Resale is the Gentlemen's Resale Corp., similarly decorated with exposed brick walls and carpet. High-end suits, sport coats, ties, dress shirts, belts, and tuxedos are available for a fraction of the retail cost.

ENCORE

$–$$

1132 Madison Ave., NYC 10028; (212) 879-2850.
Open Mon–Fri: 10:30 a.m.–6:30 p.m., Sat: 10:30 a.m.–6 p.m., Sun: noon–6 p.m.
www.EncoreResale.com

Owner: Carole Selig
Return Policy: Case by case basis
Try-on Facilities: Open dressing rooms (two on main floor and one on mezzanine)

Encore has carried the most exciting European, Asian, and American designer clothing and accessories that have belonged to some of the most notable women of our time. "Our clients are protected by our confidential treatment of their identities. However, many are quite famous."

Encore was established in 1954 and was "the first designer resale store of its kind. We have a long history of famous women consigning their designer/couture clothing to us—one of which is Jacqueline Kennedy Onassis, who started consigning with Encore in the '60s," says Selig.

Author Diana Eden used to frequent this store years ago when she lived in New York. She recalls buying a $20 Christian Dior dress just so she could take it apart to see its construction! Nowadays, it is a no-frills store, with racks and minimal attempt at display. There is a tiny corner for a few pieces of menswear, and a third floor for sportswear and accessories.

MICHAEL'S THE CONSIGNMENT SHOP FOR WOMEN

$$–$$$

1041 Madison Ave., 2nd Floor, NYC 10021; (212) 737-7273.
Open Mon–Sat: 9:30 a.m.–6 p.m. (Closed Sat during July and August)
www.MichaelsConsignment.com

Owner: Laura Fluhr
Return Policy: All sales final
Try-on Facilities: Five fitting rooms with mirrors

Michael's The Consignment Shop for Women sells both current and vintage clothing. They offer only the very highest-end designer fashions and accessories because "we are on Madison Avenue in New York and our customers expect and deserve the best."

The store, named for Fluhr's father, Michael, has been in business for 47 years; the family has been in the clothing resale business for five generations. A photo of the original turn-of-the-century store, with her great-grandfather in front and a sign reading "Cast Off Clothing/Furs" hangs near the cash register.

Today Fluhr offers: Alaïa, Anna Sui, Armani, Badgley Mischka, Ballinger-Gold, Bartlett, BCBG, Bill Blass, Bottega, Bulgari, Cartier, Calvin Klein, Céline, Chanel, Dolce & Gabbana, Oscar de la Renta, Ann Demeulemeester, Dior, Escada, Fendi, Ferragamo, Ferretti, Galliano, Gaultier, Genny, Gigli, Givenchy, Gucci, Helmut Lang, Hermès, Hindmarch, Iceberg, Inès de la Fressange, Jacobs, Jimmy Choo, Kamali, Karan, Kieselstein, Lacroix, Lagerfeld, Lauren, Lederer, Léger, Leiber, Max Mara, McFadden, McQueen, Missoni, Miyake, Morgane Le Fay, Moschino, Prada, Pucci, Robert Lee Morris, Rykiel, Scaasi, Spade, St. John, Starzewski, Trussardi, TSE, Tyler, Ungaro, Valentino, Versace, Vuitton, Yamamoto, Yurman, Zelda, and Zoran.

The most interesting piece Fluhr has ever collected? "Years ago, we took a pink brocade evening gown and coat completely lined in white mink on consignment. It was fabulous," says Fluhr. Her favorite period? "I love the '60s because the clothes were ladylike and well made."

This store sits on the second and third floors with dresses and suits downstairs, and eveningwear and wedding gowns upstairs. Wedding gowns sell for well under four figures and include labels like Vera Wang and Caroline Herrera. This shop carries only women's clothes in sizes 2–12, and will only accept garments for consignment from the list of designers posted.

There is also a small section of about two dozen pieces of very high-end designer vintage (vintage here is pre-'80s), with labels such as Halston and Galanos. Current offerings include a beautiful evening gown and matching evening coat that look straight out of the Jackie Kennedy era. Garments from this boutique have been seen in *Glitter* with Mariah Carey, *Sex and the City*, and *Family Law*.

Ritz Furs

$$$$

107 W. 57th St., NYC 10019; (212) 265-4559.
Open Mon–Sat: 9 a.m.– 6 p.m.
www.ritzfurs.com

Owner: Keith Tauber
Return Policy: All sales final
Try-on Facilities: Not needed; outerwear only

Ritz Furs has been catering to New York women who know fur for over 50 years. Tauber is famous for his ever-changing selection of fine quality pre-owned furs, including mink, fox, lamb, and even sable. Many are from famous designers, all are offered at a fraction of their original cost. This shop offers classic, traditional, contemporary, and even retro styles—today's latest trends and yesterdays fabulous finds. "Fur-trimmed capes remain a store staple and can be worn to work, dressed up for evening, or thrown over jeans for a great look," says Tauber.

There is also a wide selection of custom Ritz Collection fur-trimmed coats and jackets in precious fabrics—100 percent cashmere, alpaca, and loden, all trimmed with luxurious fox or mink. A selection of warm and elegant fur-lined coats is also available, as well as shearlings, leather coats, and jackets. Opulent fur collars, cuffs, boas, fur-trimmed gloves, headbands, bags, and more are offered in a wide range of colors like red, blue, pumpkin, and green. Don't miss their "Downstairs at the Ritz" showroom offering a huge selection of great retro, vintage, funky, and fun furs.

The most interesting piece collected by Tauber? A sable coat, named "Freddie" by its first owner, that resold for $19,000. Current offerings include: a beautiful sable coat with shawl collar, straight sleeves, and a Revillon label; a blue mink coat with notch collar and belt with a Bergdorf Goodman label; and their own precious fiber outerwear coats (cashmere, alpaca, loden, and microfiber) with removable liners made from pre-owned mink.

TATIANA'S

$$$

767 Lexington Ave., 5th Floor, NYC 10021; (212) 755-7744.
Open Mon–Sat: 11 a.m.–7 p.m.
www.Tatianas.com

> **Owner:** Tatiana
> **Return Policy:** Case by case basis
> **Try-on Facilities:** Dressing room

Tatiana's is a small, romantic store on the Upper East Side that's been in business for four years, offering high-end designer and vintage couture. This shop features nicely displayed suits and garments by Dolce & Gabbana, Thierry Mugler, Jill Stuart, Prada, Gucci, Chanel, Valentino, Versace, and Hermès. They also offer designer dresses—including gowns previously worn to the Academy Awards—Chanel couture from the 1960s–80s, lots of shoes organized according to size, day and evening purses, silk scarves, and some jewelry. The contemporary resale is gathered from Tatiana's upscale clientele, fashion models, and showrooms.

The most interesting piece Tatiana has collected is a 1956 Christian Dior gown. Just how much does Tatiana love her work? "My husband told me if I buy any more designerwear he'll leave me…I am going to miss him."

Additional Resale Stores

Fisch for the Hip: 153 W. 18th St., NYC 10011; (212) 633-9053.

INA: 101 Thompson St., NYC 10012; (212) 941-4757.

Off Broadway Boutique: 139 W. 72nd St., 1st Floor, NYC 10023; (212) 724-6713.

A Second Chance Designer: 1109 Lexington Ave., 2nd Floor, NYC 10021; (212) 744-6041.

major retailers that carry vintage

Barney's Melrose Avenue Decades: 660 Madison Ave., NYC 10021; (212) 826-8900.

DKNY: 655 Madison Ave., NYC 10021; (212) 223-DKNY(3569).

DKNY: 420 W. Broadway, NYC 10012; (646) 613-1100.

Double RL: 271 Mulberry St., NYC 10012; (212) 343-0841.

Norma Kamali: 11 W. 56th St., NYC 10019; (212) 957-9797.

Betsey Johnson: 138 Wooster St., NYC 10012; (212) 995-5048.

Jill Stuart: 100 Greene St., NYC 10012; (212) 343-2300.

Reaction Kenneth Cole: 130 E. 57th St., NYC 10022; (212) 688-1670.

Tommy Hilfiger: 372 W. Broadway, NYC 10012; (917) 237-0983.

Prada Guggenheim: 575 Broadway, NYC 10012; (212) 334-8888

AMERICAN VINTAGE CLASSICS

$$

www.geocities.com/american_vintage_classics

> *Owner:* Rico Giordano
> *Return Policy:* Refund within one week

American Vintage Classics claims to be the world's largest web site for men's vintage clothing and carries a limited selection of women's wear and accessories. They specialize in exceptional American vintage from the post-war '40s to the mid-'50s, and serve 2,000 customers from all over the world. This Internet store boasts a gigantic guest book of vintage lovers from all around the planet, including Finnish costume designer, Jorma Honkanen. With simple text and pictures, it's not fancy but has everything a vintage clothing buyer wants, like good sizing information, clothing descriptions, and conditions of the items. Included in their stock are several hundred shirts and ties, which are available on-line daily. Current women's stock includes a hand-screened cream-colored Minklander by Darlene sweater with an orange and brown flower motif made from lambswool, fur, and nylon.

Owner's favorite period is the '40s—specifically wide swing ties worn with rayon gabardine slacks and shirts.

ANGELICA'S ATTIC

$

www.angelicasattic.com

> *Owner:* Deni Sinnott
> *Return Policy:* Refund within one week for size only

Angelica's Attic specializes in dresses, coats, and blouses, because "dresses can help you make a fun statement with color and fabric, and blouses can easily be integrated into the rest of your wardrobe," says Sinnott. The most interesting piece Sinnott has personally collected is a black caftan with ostrich feathers on the sleeves that is "very mysterious, it could also double as a Halloween costume." Sinnott's favorite period is the '70s, "when the color of the '60s met practical design concepts; lots of fun polyester and huge collars!"

Scouting vintage stores, estate sales, flea markets, and the closets of clothes lovers for stock, Sinnott carries St. John, Gucci, and Bill Blass—just to name a few. Current stock includes: cotton dresses with side zippers; fun prints from the '50s; polyester specials with loud colors and designs that have "eye poker-outer" collars; blouses that combine beautifully with new jeans and have great retro buttons; and furry and fun coats with style and color that you won't find in your neighborhood mall.

ANTIQUE & VINTAGE DRESS GALLERY

$$–$$$

www.antiquedress.com

> **Owner:** Deborah Burke
> **Return Policy:** Refund on items over $150 within two days, less shipping

Antique & Vintage Dress Gallery opened in 1997. Burke had been working as an executive recruiter and hated her job. With a 25-year collection of antique and vintage clothing and $500 set aside for a web site designer, Burke started her virtual shop with 30 items for sale. Today Burke carries top antique, vintage, and Hollywood designers from the 1800s to the 1980s. These include Charles Worth, Emile Pingat, Jacques Doucet, Callot Soeurs, Ceil Chapman, Pauline Trigére, Bonnie Cashin, Jacques Fath, Balenciaga, Howard Greer, Irene, Helen Rose, Bob Mackie, Bes-Ben, Christian Dior, Rudi Gernreich, Bill Blass, Valentino, Emilio Pucci, Lilli Ann, and Galanos.

"Ever since I was a little girl, I wanted to work as a designer/costumer in the movie biz. However, I can't draw and I can't sew and, frankly, I really can't design, so that career sort of seemed out of the question for me. What

I can do is recognize great design, great fabrics, great quality goods from truly great fashion and Hollywood designers. My web site has afforded me the opportunity to have those pieces pass through my fingers.

"I have the greatest customers, but perhaps two of my more unusual sales include the male cross-dresser in Finland who purchased an original Edwardian woman's corset, and an English gentleman seeking a 'Mrs. Robinson' outfit. It's customers like that who make my days so much fun! I'm a collector at heart myself, so I pride myself in knowing what customers will like. That's my joy."

Burke specializes in antique and vintage fancy and/or finely tailored garments, that are mainly for women, but also carries contemporary designers such as Armani, Galanos, Escada, Lacroix, and Thierry Mugler. She scours the world to find pieces in excellent condition. She usually sells wearable items but also sells many items to collectors. "The clothing of today just can't come close to the beauty in every stitch, detail, and line of antique and vintage clothes. The most interesting piece I have ever collected is a post-Titanic era men's fine wool suit vest, which is actually a life vest! For the man who wanted to look well-dressed while on a cruise ship—and yet smartly prepared for possible disaster!" Burke's personal favorites? Edwardian ball gowns for their combination of fancy detail trims and sophisticated lines.

Current offerings include: a circa 1944 black chiffon overdress, once owned by Mrs. J. D. Rockefeller, that is flared at the bottom and decorated with bands of sequins over a black, stiff taffeta slip with scalloped hemline; a circa 1880s/1890s House of Worth couture bottle green silk velvet beaded capelet with black lace; and an 1820s sky blue, silk ball gown with coral, silk trim.

"Clothes are things that people should collect. A beautiful garment can work forever if it works on you—fit is everything. Evening clothes, especially, have no period— a wonderful fit, unique details, and a flattering neckline last forever."

—BOB MACKIE

ANTIQUE LACE & FASHION

$$$

www.antique-fashion.com

> *Owner:* Karen Augusta
> *Return Policy:* Refund within 24 hours

Antique Lace & Fashion carries a variety of designers, including Charles Worth, Emile Pingat, Galenga, Chanel, Adrian, Irene, Dior, and Mainbocher which Augusta has acquired from private customers, antique dealers, and auctions. She also has beautifully made, museum-quality clothing and accessories from the 18th century through 1950, and also collects 18th-century stays (corsets). Her favorite period is the early 20th century because "the dramatic changes in Western women's fashion of the period are directly related to advances they were making in society," says Augusta.

Augusta has "loaned" clothing to stylists working for Courtney Love, Madonna, and others. Her pieces have been featured in *Vanity Fair, Vogue Hommes, Mademoiselle,* and *Victoria* magazines. She also sells to many well-known fashion designers, such as Donna Karan, Adrienne Vittadini, and Mary McFadden. Augusta provided many of the early 20th-century garments and accessories to Deborah Scott and Lahly Poore of Columbia for the film *Titanic.* After receiving these pieces back, she loaned them out again for *The Patriot.*

AZILLION SPARKLZ

$–$$$$

www.sparklz.com

> *Owner:* Janet W. Lawwill
> *Return Policy:* Refund within seven days

Azillion SPARKLZ does indeed sparkle with antique and vintage costume and fine gemstone jewelry including rhinestone, Victorian pieces, Bakelite and other plastic jewelry, sterling silver, compacts, perfumes, mesh and beaded bags, cufflinks, tie tacs, bracelets, bracelet and necklace charms, earrings, and rings. You will find diamonds, colored stones, coral, platinum, and gold acquired from individuals, resale shops, antique stores, and other sources.

Lawwill counts costume designers and celebrities as clients, including "Demi Moore, who shopped my mall space in New Mexico."

BARBARA'S BACKROOM
$$

www.barbp.win.net

> *Owner:* Barbara Phipps
> *Return Policy:* Refund within 24 hours less shipping

Barbara's Backroom specializes in wearable 1920s–70s. "I love to look elegant and different from everyone else," says Phipps. To that end, her stock includes her personal collection of vintage clothing, 450 hats, hat boxes, hatpins, and accessories collected from travels around the U.S., to estate sales, vintage stores, flea markets, auctions, friends, and neighbors. She ships all around the world, from Chicago, New York, and Los Angeles to Hong Kong and the United Kingdom.

The most interesting piece Phipps personally has collected is a designer hat autographed and personally fitted by milliner Frank Olive during Derby week in Louisville, Kentucy.

Sandra Bullock accessorized a gown with 19th-century vintage diamonds from Fred Leighton for the 2002 Oscars

"Elegance is a question of personality, more than one's clothing."
—JEAN PAUL GAULTIER

CAROLINE'S CLOSETS

$$

www.carolinescloset.com

Owner: Caroline Keating
Return Policy: Store credit within one week

Caroline's Closets' Caroline Keating believes that vintage goodies have stories gently worn into their flashback fabrics. "Whether personal or historical," says Keating, "we try to pass along as much as we know about each item to our customers. We are dedicated to serving up 'history with the hip.' We're on a mission to recycle and reclaim past treasures and polish them up with personal stories in the hope of reinforcing a sense of community. As we play matchmaker between cast off clothes and an audience of voracious vintage friends, we funnel ten percent of our profits to local and national non-profit organizations. Working closely with the Di Di Hirsch Community Mental Health center in LA, we see firsthand how a piece of old clothing helps bring much-needed peace to others."

The good karma seems to be working; pristine Emilio Pucci, Lilly Pulitzer, Oscar de la Renta, Jeanne Lanvin, Courrèges, and Vera Wang pieces land on her doorstep. Julia Roberts reportedly wore one of the Pucci pieces.

"Since our launch we've gained a name for carrying a classic, ever growing collection of Lilly Pulitzer as well as Vera Wang and Pucci prints. I like creating a 'flashback experience' for our customers and specialize in pieces that scream a certain era. My joy in finding a Day-Glo 'Frankie Says Relax' T-shirt is no less intense than the rush of finding a mind-blowing Gernreich scarf. We're not driven by worth but in how much it can 'bring you back.'"

The most interesting piece Keating has ever collected? "My Lilly Pulitzer smiling bumblebee golf skirt. It was my first intro to the 'print-cess' of Palm Beach and I wore it for inspiration as I tried to channel the Lilly spirit and boldly paint my own future. When I tracked her down at a local Lilly trunk show and told her of my vintage passion and plans she called me 'brave' but not for embracing the entrepreneurial spirit—instead for the courage it must take to 'wear her '70s prints in public'. I've kept the smiling bumblebees close at hand ever since and wear them as a cloak of courage whenever I need a boost."

Current offerings include: the "Star Spangled Butterfly" silk blouse in vibrant shades of red, white, and blue from the Vera Wang "All-American Collection"; a Van Halen "1984 Tour of the World" silkscreen T-shirt (classic baseball style tee in white with black sleeve); and an Emilio Pucci '60s silk matte jersey in swirls of chartreuse, olive, asparagus, periwinkle, tangerine, and hot pink—a kaleidoscope of color with smoked crystal beadwork dangling from the belt end.

THE CATS PAJAMAS
$$

www.catspajamas.com

> **Owner:** Laura Hauze
> **Return Policy:** Refund within three days less 10% restocking fee

The Cats Pajamas offers vintage clothing and accessories from the Victorian era to the '70s. Located in Williamsport since 1987, this web site offers a huge amount of stock. You've seen their goods in *From the Earth to the Moon, Tales of the City, Little Women, Inventing Abbotts, As Good as it Gets, Town and Country, Riding in Cars With Boys,* and more. Hauze supplied around 6,000 '30s and '40s outfits for *Come See the Paradise.*

Designers carried include Schiaparelli, Daché, Lilly Pulitzer, Mr. John, Geoffrey Beene, and Hattie Carnegie. Owner "Miss Kitty" loves offering clothes from the '40s, but a full line of every era is available. She is especially proud of their Charles Worth (Victorian) pieces.

JENNIFER LOPEZ **at her new restaurant, Madre's, in Pasadena, California in 2002 in vintage John Anthony.**

Circa-1900

$

www.circa-1900.com or www.winelady.com

> **Owner:** Patty Cole and Paul Grothem
> **Return Policy:** Refund within five days

Circa-1900 specializes in reproduction vintage and Victorian items as well as genuine vintage gathered from estate sales. The web site changes often with new items constantly available—wholesale pricing is offered on many pieces. "We are avid collectors who peruse estate sales and auctions all over the Midwest. One of our finds was a fantastic collection of over 1,000 vintage hats. With the addition of accessories, our web site took off," says Cole and Grothem.

Cole and Grothem's most interesting pieces are hats worn by Charlie Chaplin, Mary Pickford, Gloria Swanson, and Marlene Dietrich. Favorite period? The fabulous Roaring Twenties when people enjoyed a boom economy that was reflected in lavish cars and parties. Current offerings include: Mary Pickford's burgundy touring hat, wonderfully designed with flowers and lace and in excellent condition; and a Roberta Bernay feather cloche with peacock feathers applied by hand.

The Daisy Shop

$$–$$$

www.daisyshop.com

> **Owner:** Barbara Abarbanell
> **Return Policy:** All sales final

The Daisy Shop has it all! Vintage designers carried include Chanel, Valentino, Gucci, Louis Vuitton, Pierre Balmain, Pucci, Givenchy, Ben Reig, Ben Zuckerman, Pauline Trigère, Hanae Mori, Becky Bisoulis, Bob Mackie, Halston, Mollie Parnis, Donald Brooks, Adolfo, Bes-Ben, Ciner, Weiss,

Eisenberg, Stefan Lissner, Susan Kramer, Dominique Aurentis, Jacob Javits, Oscar de la Renta, Dior, Judith Leiber, Helga Wagner, Ilie Wacs, Burberry, and Jean Muir.

Contemporary resale includes Chanel, Valentino, Gucci, Louis Vuitton, Armani, Commes des Garçons, Yamamoto, Escada, St. John, Marc Jacobs, Jil Sander, Oscar de la Renta, Christian Lacroix, Miu Miu, Anna Sui, Galliano, Missoni, Versace, Yves Saint Laurent, Dior, Remi Lagos, Janis Savitt, Kieselstein-Cord, Prada, Ferragamo, Martin Margiela, Jacques Fath, Hanae Mori, Judith Leiber, Burberry, Dennis Basso, and Lagerfeld.

Abarbanell has specialized in vintage couture clothing and accessories and signed costume jewelry since opening in June 1995. "Vintage merchandise complements our contemporary couture clothing and accessories," says Abarbanell. "The most interesting pieces I've collected so far include: a Hermés 'Prairie Flowers' scarf; a Dinicola faux garnet, turquoise, and pearl domed pin; a Madame Grés black silk jersey-draped daywear dress; and a German silver mesh reticule circa 1890." Abarbanell's personal weakness is for cashmere twin sets, specifically 3 and 4 ply by the masters Ballantyne, Jean-Louis Scherrer, and Phyllis Dalton. Current offerings include a Gina LaMendola long-sleeved ball gown worked in three different silk fabrics with a V-neck and circle skirt.

Abarbanell's quest began when one day in 1995 she happened upon a severely abused, moth ridden, red and blue striped wool jersey Chanel suit tagged $13. "The sleeve and its clearly identifiable Chanel button caught my eye. I bought it in a moment, along with each and every other couture item I could find until my 'starter' store opened on June 10, 1995.

"I renovated that Chanel, reconditioned it, had every moth hole repaired, replaced the lining, shortened the skirt, and wore it for a publicity shoot at the kickoff of my store. I can't tell you why I choose it, but the suit has become my uniform. I never tire of wearing it. I don't know who purchased this suit originally from Chanel, but I know she was a small-framed, lean person, for the suit is small, and only thin women are willing to wear horizontal stripes!"

Dandelion Vintage Clothing

$$$

www.dandelion-vintage.com

> **Owner:** Carol Baker
> **Return Policy:** All sales final

Dandelion Vintage Boutique sells vintage clothing and accessories from the Victorian era to the '70s. There is a wide variety of dresses, including plus sizes, from casual, dressy, or black to informal wedding gowns. There is also a large lingerie department and a nice selection of seamed stockings that were old store stock.

Baker's personal love is loungewear and pajamas from the '20s and '30s, such as long embroidered robes, wide legged silk pants, and tunic tops and slippers edged with feathers. She has silk floral pajamas and kimono robes from that era hanging in her home. Her favorite period is the 1930s–40s because of the great fabrics and styles.

Current stock includes: a green and black Roman-print (helmets, griffins, and square spirals) peach dress of the 1940s–50s; a '30s rosy brocade gown; and a L'Elegance, hand-sewn peach rayon 1930s–40s bias cut nightgown with white lace straps that ties at the waist.

Davenport and Company

$$

www.davenportandco.com

> **Owner:** Dee Davenport-Howe
> **Return Policy:** Refund within three days less 10% restocking fee

Davenport and Company owner Davenport-Howe has been collecting vintage for at least 30 years from vintage shows, estate sales, vintage shops, and antique sales. "I couldn't stop buying, so I decided to start selling," says Davenport-Howe. "I opened a shop and went on-line at the same time; half the money pays my expenses and the other half supports my wildlife rehab center. I take in orphaned and injured wild mammals and release them into the wild once they're able to fend for themselves. So anyone buying is helping baby raccoons, skunks, squirrels, opossums, and other small animals."

Current offerings include: a two-piece Edwardian wedding gown in cream organdy and silk with lace trim, hemmed with off-white velvet; a '30s blue-green and navy silk check dress with long narrow sleeves, a large pointed satin collar with a bow, and four deco rhinestone closures in front; and an 1870–80s three-piece bodice, skirt, and overskirt in copper and black striped silk with black silk trim on collar, hem, cuffs, and sleeve seams.

DRESSHOPNYC

$$

www.dresshopnyc.com

> *Owner:* Michele Peress
> *Return Policy:* Refund within three days less 15% restocking fee

Dresshopnyc specializes in women's designer vintage clothing and other unique pieces dating from the 1930s–70s with occasional special items from other eras. Peress began selling unique vintage pieces that she picked up on various photography trips around the country. "I'd sell them to friends at art school, at parties, or right out of my school bag. After school, I moved to New York and opened Dresshopnyc on the Internet. What interests me about the Internet is that the clothes can be sold all over, in small towns, in big cities, in various countries," says Peress. "I have been collecting and selling vintage clothing for several years now, and it continues to be a source of infinite fascination and excitement for the insight it provides into history. I believe vintage clothing offers a freedom in the way we think about clothing and promises an expression of individuality to the wearer."

The designers carried in this shop depend on current stock at any given time, as Peress is not loyal to any one decade or any one particular designer. Rather than specializing in a particular style of clothing, she chooses items for originality, quality of construction, and how well a garment has been cared for and preserved.

She sells only pieces that are in "excellent to mint condition." Designers carried include Pauline Trigère, Halston, Yves Saint Laurent, Pierre Balmain, Ossie Clark, Biba, Lilly Pulitzer, Diane von Furstenberg, Jeanne Lanvin, Mary Quant, Zandra Rhodes, Jean Muir, Roberta di Camerino, Giorgio di Saint'Angelo, Alaïa, Schiaparelli, Hattie Carnegie, Helen Rose, Koos van den Akker, Leonard, Estevez, Geoffrey Beene, Pucci, Hanae Mori, Claire McCardell, Norman Norell, and Betsey Johnson.

"I can fall in love with a single aspect of a garment," says Peress, "a luxurious fabric, exquisite draping, expert tailoring, or unique details. I have always had a soft spot for the glamour of the '30s: accentuated backs, bias cut draping, rich fabrics. I am also enamored by the designs of the '70s, which find their inspiration in the '30s in the fabric, detail, and construction. I find it intriguing to witness the reinterpretation of one designer's point of view by another. Style and design are constantly being invented and reinvented."

Items currently in stock include: a '40s Lilli Ann Original two-piece gabardine suit in forest green with an accompanying belt; a '50s Ceil Chapman dress with beautiful floral lace over a flesh tone lining; and a '70s Christian Dior for Saks Fifth Avenue black crêpe dress with a mock wrap bodice, sexy plunging neckline, and slim skirt.

"If you're buying recycled or vintage clothes and the tag has been removed, take it to a good dry cleaner. Sometimes they can determine the fiber content."

—JEANNINE STEIN, *LOS ANGELES TIMES*, MARCH 29, 2002

1860–1960 ONE HUNDRED YEARS OF FASHION & ACCESSORIES

$$

www.1860-1960.com

> **Owner:** Beth and Julie Guernsey
> **Return Policy:** Refund within three days less shipping

1860–1960 One Hundred Years of Fashion & Accessories is a mother-and-daughter team who have been in the vintage clothing business for almost 30 years, dealing in clothing and accessories from 1860 to 1960. Their favorite periods are the Victorian and Edwardian eras, because clothing was romantic and well-constructed.

Current offerings include: a yellow cotton floral day dress from about 1920 with a raised floral appliqué pattern along the front and back and cub work design around the skirt, arms, and down the front of the top; a pair of orange silk embroidered shoes measuring nine inches long and three inches wide from the '20s; and a sensational silver mesh purse from about 1915, marked inside by the clasp "Silver 800."

The Guernseys have worked with costume designers Deborah Scott, Colleen Atwood, and Judianna Makovsky for such films as *Titanic, Little Women, Beloved,* and *The Legend of Bagger Vance.*

ENOKIWORLD

$$–$$$

www.enokiworld.com

> **Owner:** Madeline Meyerowitz
> **Return Policy:** Refund within ten days less 10% restocking fee

Enokiworld carries everything from '30s Robert Piguet to '80s Christian Lacroix, but Meyerowitz's primary focus is on designer vintage clothing and accessories from the '60s and '70s. "We have a little bit of everything from deco to punk, but we find ourselves most interested in women designers as they bring a sympathetic aspect to the table. Who better to design for a woman than another woman? We also believe in bringing forward obscure designer names and labels that have gone relatively unnoticed."

The most interesting piece Meyerowitz has ever collected? "That's a quirky question," says Meyerowitz. "I might say something like a Courrèges fleece coat this week and then next week, a woman will walk in with a Christian Dior green and yellow dyed mink from the '60s and I would think that was absolutely it. The nature of the vintage clothing business is so serendipitous—you never know what is around the corner—so not only is your inventory changing, but our tastes as buyers and our favorite pieces are as well. There are designers I am consistently in love with though: Jean-Charles de Castelbajac, André Courrèges, Bonnie Cashin, John Anthony."

Meyerowitz's favorite period is the '60s, "because the political change within those years makes one decade seem like two. You started out riding on the prim and proper coattails of the '50s and then, with the Vietnam war and the introduction of the birth control pill, things took a 180-degree turn as we headed toward the '70s. The changes of the '60s are reflected in fashion more than any other time."

By the way, "most people," says Meyerowitz, "use the term 'couture' erroneously, meaning anything designer, but couture is a term reserved for items that have been custom-made for a particular woman, although they range anywhere from tailor-made to straight from the atelier of a well-respected house, like Dior."

Current offerings include a '60s Bonnie Cashin sand-colored leather coat. "The strength of Bonnie Cashin's work lies in its ability to harmonize with all of the other pieces in her collections. They don't vastly differ from year to year, and they all flow together beautifully. And while some people are not jumping up and down over Cashin's work because they seek something that is totally trendy and over-the-top, Cashin is in the same group of creative thinkers as Andy Warhol and Pablo Picasso."

FashionDig.com
$–$$$

www.fashiondig.com

> *Owner:* Janet Pytowski and Barry Bryant, Co-Founders
> *Return Policy:* Varies from vendor to vendor

Fashiondig.com specializes in the 1900s–1980s, but Pytowski and Bryant's favorite period is the mid to late '60s. The most interesting piece they have ever collected is a '60s Courrèges dress.

Billed as "the most stylish fashion and vintage design site on the web," this site explores 20th-century style, offering links to shopping sites. Browse this site for image archives, hot collectibles, and fashion advice. Share your thoughts and ideas with other "Fashion Diggers." They also offer a book-shop, fashion forum, and "Ask Janet," an interactive source for questions and answers. Other features include "My Closet," where fashion aficionados can buy, sell, or trade clothes, and FashionDig's classified section for the style savvy shopper. Want know exactly how to "have a mode wedding," or how to have your hair cut "exactly like Marilyn Monroe"? Ask Janet, the omniscient style authority at FashionDig, a cyberspace mall of stores, articles, photographs, and forums.

Justsaywhen
$–$$$

www.justsaywhen.com

> *Owner:* Milan Tainan
> *Return Policy:* Refund within seven days less shipping

Justsaywhen carries a cornucopia of designers including Bill Blass, Chanel, Halston, Pauline Trigère, Hanae Mori, Norman Norell, Gucci, Emilio Pucci, Vera Maxwell, Stephen Burrows, Giorgio di Sant'Angelo, Mary McFadden, Vicky Tiel, Diane Freis, Marimekko, Missoni, Armani, Byblos, Issey Miyake,

Valentino, Stavropoulos, Mollie Parnis, Norma Kamali, Scaasi, and Victor Costa, gathered from flea markets, thrift stores, other vintage dealers, Tainan's mom, and individuals around the world.

Tainan specializes in beautiful vintage items that may or may not have a designer label. All items are either never worn or in mint, excellent, or very good condition. "My vintage items are meant to be worn and enjoyed, so we don't sell any seriously damaged items or any items meant just for display."

The most interesting piece Tainan has collected is a 1968 never-worn "Givenchy gown, with the original price tag of $4,432 still attached. I sold it to Zoe Tay, a famous Asian actress, who wore it as her wedding gown. My favorite period is the '30s for bias cut dresses, '40s for superbly tailored suits, and '70s for its gypsy, romantic, I-don't-give-a-damn fashion attitude."

The web site is currently offering a rare 1969 Geoffrey Beene velvet mini-dress, with a black silk-lined bodice and a black silk organza skirt. "His designs, from the beginning, were always youthful with a certain doll-like quality—empire-waisted, short or long, dresses fashioned like jumpers, adorned with what we now refer to as very 'Beene' bands of braids or ribbons. 'Relaxed elegance' is a term that is often used to describe his masterful creations. This dress is part of his highest priced collections…which the designer himself labeled 'couture' for its quality, rather than because of custom fitting, which is normally only considered couture."

Also in stock is a '60s Oscar de la Renta for Jane Derby, "from Oscar de la Renta's earliest American design period. It wasn't until 1974, when Oscar bought the Jane Derby company (which he had been designing for since the mid-60s), that the label bore his name alone. This dress is magical; a beautiful pink silk faille completely covered with small silver discs and metallic silver thread interwoven into the fabric—they are not appliqués or pasted on. There are so many haute couture elements to this piece I just get goose bumps."

"Isn't elegance forgetting what one is wearing?"
—YVES SAINT LAURENT

ML VINTAGE
$$–$$$

www.meredith.com.au
PAYMENT BY DRAFT ONLY

> *Owner:* Mary Lipshut
> *Return Policy:* All sales final

ML Vintage offers Missoni, Pucci, Walter Albini, Courrèges, Versace, Callaghan, Genny—with a very unusual twist. "In the late '60s, '70s, and early '80s," says Lipshut, "the company Meredith Group Ltd. was the sole importer of these designer labels. I had exclusive representation and imported for the whole of Australia, and because of this, today I can offer never worn Courréges from 1973, for example, because that enitre shipment arrived one week after France tested the first bomb in the Pacific and Australia black-banned everything French for such a long time that by the time I received my shipment some two years later, it was totally out of date. On the advice of friends in Milan, I packed it away, forgotten until now."

It was in 1996 that the full extent of the collection became apparent. The collection was enormous and included new garments and accessories from vintage collections of over 25 different designers including Gianni Versace (1978–82) (his own label, as well as Versace for Callaghan (1972–78), Genny (1976–82), and Complice (1975–77)), Missoni (1971–83), Courrèges (1971–74), Basile (1974–82), Pucci (1971–73), Roberta di Camerino (1972–74), Walter Albini for Misterfox (1970–71), Nina Ricci Jewelry (1973–74), and many more. But probably the most amazing aspect of the Meredith Vintage Collection is that the garments are all brand new, many with original hangtags and protective wrappings. Collectors from around the world are starting to realize that the Meredith Vintage collection may yet prove to be one of the most important collections of 20th-century designer fashion.

Lipshut's personal collection includes the first Missoni she ever bought in 1967. "Interesting, because it was one of the few pieces designed for Missoni by the French designer Emmanuele Khan. Both names are in the woven label. This garment is in the National Museum of Victoria." Her favorite era is "definitely the '70s. Every season there was something new and exciting. Above all, women were well dressed and elegant. Opening nights at the theater were exciting fashion parades."

Current offerings include: a white satin cocktail coat by Walter Albini for Misterfox; a pure silk, printed, jersey evening gown by Missoni; and an evening set by Courrèges with a completely see-through top, with rib neck and cuffs, and a long wool skirt accented with a vinyl waistband, bow, and hem.

NANCY'S NIFTY NOOK VINTAGE CLOTHING

$$

www.nancysniftynook.com

> ***Owner:*** Nancy Stoner
> ***Return Policy:*** Store credit within five days

Nancy's Nifty Nook Vintage Clothing sells a variety of vintage clothing, from the mid-'60s—or mod era—back to the Victorian period, including coats and furs. They also have an interesting $9.99 division, which sells more modern collectable vintage from the late '60s to the '90s.

One of the most interesting pieces Stoner sold was a "fabulous Victorian dress from the mid-1800s, most certainly the Civil War era and in perfect condition, to a customer in Japan." Her favorite period is the '40s. "I just love those big linebacker shoulder pads and flared swingy skirts—such style and grace, something not around today!"

Current offerings include: a '40s David Roth Original, "knock out, drop dead gorgeous, to die for" black silk satin dress with round neckline, full-length dolman sleeves; a high quality wool dress in deep wine with a cowl neckline, X-stitched bodice, and matching jacket of gray faux Persian lamb from the '40s; and a full-length, swing-style, brown beaver coat with a small tuxedo-style collar and full-length sleeves that have elastic in the wrist area to snug them up.

NEEN'S ANTIQUE & VINTAGE CLOTHING

$–$$$

www.neens.com

> **Owner:** Jeanine Fenwick Murphy
> **Return Policy:** Refund within three days

Neen's Antique & Vintage Clothing caters to shoppers from all over the world, offering vintage designer and couture. Unique and high-quality construction is their specialty, according to Murphy, and special requests are always welcome as the items shown on the site are only a very small percentage of Neen's Stock.

Some of Neen's clients are vintage dealers that seek hard to find and special items for their own clients. Murphy plays host once a year to many vintage vendors who come together for the ultimate in vintage clothing shopping. She and husband Paul are promoters of the Northwest Vintage Expo held annually in Portland, Oregon. See their web site calendar for scheduled vintage shows across the country.

Murphy specializes in Victorian–1950s, with a limited selection from the '60s and '70s. The most interesting pieces she has collected are "Phyllis Diller's French lace flapper dress, two wide brim hats that belonged to Lucille Ball, and an ivory handmade lace Victorian ball gown, with Shanghai couture label, that belonged to the last surviving member of the Whitman Indian Massacre."

Murphy's favorite period is the '30s through mid-'40s when "designers were trying to out-design each other with classy and wild deco creations.

Most importantly, flattering the body was high priority. Bias cut dresses transformed imperfections to perfection."

Current offerings include: a handmade, French, black silk Edwardian dress of impeccable Novelle styling; a green and clear rhinestone chiffon dress from the '20s or early '30s; and a '40s navy wool gabardine suit with unique deco influenced lapels.

NICOLE'S REVIVAL

$–$$$$

www.nicolesrevival.com

Owner: Nicole Schneider
Return Policy: Case by case basis

Nicole's Revival specializes in business suits, from less expensive to high-end designers, including the Gap, J.Crew, Donna Karan, Chanel, Giorgio Armani, DKNY, Escada, and Liz Claiborne. "We're entering our ninth year in business and are a regular donor (of all profits) to many local charities."

Owner Nicole Schneider offers local and European resale bus tours. Participants board a bus and travel first class, visiting resale shops for the day. "These tours are what made Nicole's Revival famous. It started with local tours which got so big they now sell out within a week of announcing the date. We now have national as well as European tours." Schneider hosted the first ever European resale tour to London and Paris in the fall of 1999. Schneider also produces fashion shows and teaches fashion classes in Westland, Michigan, area schools. Her favorite find? "A Swarovski crystal beaded bag by Judith Leiber—just gorgeous!"

The web site has well over 300 items regularly featured; current offerings include: a Giorgio Armani man's gray and taupe herringbone cashmere suit; a Turnbull & Asserman's blue and white gingham-check cotton shirt; and a ladies' St. John wool and black rayon eveningwear jacket and skirt.

THE OLD LACE AND LINEN SHOP

$$

www.antiquelinen.com

> ***Owner:*** Anna MacPhail
> ***Return Policy:*** Refund within three days less 15% restocking

The Old Lace and Linen Shop specializes in antique and period clothing with designers such as Hermès and Dior. MacPhail shops the British Isles for stock. Her favorite period is the romantic Victorian era (1837–1901). One of her most interesting finds is a "fabulous christening gown from Austrian royalty."

Current offerings include: a '50s Christian Dior gold metallic gown; Saks Fifth Avenue '30s peach silk underwear; and an 1890 Chinese silk embroidered kimono. MacPhail's wares have been seen in the films *Interview With the Vampire*, *Evita*, *Rob Roy*, and *The Wings of the Dove*.

RED ROSE
VINTAGE CLOTHING

$$

www.rrnspace.com

> ***Owner:*** Don and Daphne Harris
> ***Return Policy:*** Refund within three days less shipping

Red Rose Vintage Clothing specializes in Victorian–1970s clothing gathered from estates and private collectors. The Harris' like wearable vintage clothing from the '40s but also appreciate gorgeous items from the '20s and earlier. Most important, they "like selling clothing to be worn, not just admired in a collection."

The most interesting piece collected? "Wow! That's a toughie!" says Harris. "I've had designer originals, silk Suzy Perette formals, a floral print hand-sewn dress from 1838; a black Lucite box purse covered in rhinestones—

many treasures in a 20-plus year career." Their favorite era is the '40s for "dressmaker tailored suits, sexy ankle strap platform shoes, whimsical handbags, crazy hats—an all-around fabulous look!"

Current stock includes: a '50s cream-colored cashmere cardigan with an autumn haze mink collar; a '40s tailored dressmaker suit with bound buttonholes by Peck and Peck; and a '40s Fred Astaire-style tail suit in wool and rayon faille. Their clothes were worn in A *League of Their Own, Eight Men Out, Legend of Bagger Vance,* and others.

REFLECTIONS IN VINTAGE CLOTHING

$$

www.shoporium.com/shops/treasuresyoucanwear

> ***Owner:*** Wayne and Bernice Richard
> ***Return Policy:*** Refund within three days

Reflections in Vintage Clothing specializes in formal, business, and wedding wear and offers the likes of Schiaparelli and Yves Saint Laurent. The Richards love dresses with rhinestones and '40s wedding gowns. The most interesting piece they have ever collected was an 1830s wedding gown "that was going to be thrown into the trash." Their favorite period is the 1920s–50s for elegant, classic, feminine looks.

REFLECTIONS OF THE PAST, ANTIQUE MARKETPLACE

$$–$$$

www.victoriana.com *or* www.victoriana.com/antique-marketplace

> ***Owner:*** Joanne Haug
> ***Return Policy:*** Refund within three days less shipping

Reflections of the Past, Antique Marketplace's owner, Joanne Haug, has traveled the world of auctions, estate sales, dealers, and collectors to bring her 18th-century–1920s garments, lace, linens, textiles, and needlework to you. This web site offers over 20 categories of merchandise with large color images.

Although the most interesting piece Haug has ever collected was an 1880s Charles Worth evening gown, which she donated to the Cincinnati Art Museum, her favorite period is the Regency era, because "I find the simple, elegant lines the most attractive style of any period." For her personal collection, she loves children's fashion from the 1690s to the 1950s.

Haug has had pieces on exhibit at the Valentine Museum in Richmond, Virginia and the DAR in Washington, D.C., and has sold pieces to many other museums including the Smithsonian National Postal Museum, the Smithsonian National Museum of American History, the Bata Shoe Museum (Toronto), the Colonial Williamsburg, Conner Prairie (Indiana), the Indianapolis Children's Museum, Parks Canada, the Rishon-Le Zion Museum (Israel), and the Balbriggan Historical Society (Ireland).

....

RETRODRESS
$–$$$

ww.retrodress.com

> **Owner:** Laureen Redden
> **Return Policy:** Within ten days less 15% restocking

Retrodress specializes in designer labels and unique no-name pieces because, according to Redden, vintage apparel reflects "an attention to detail that, for the most part, is sorely lacking in today's throwaway world. But I always have an eye out for pieces that may not be a designer name yet are unique, quirky, or just fun to add that perfect touch of spice to one's wardrobe."

Redden's fascination with vintage clothing began at an early age, and was fostered by her mother, who would take her on shopping trips to thrift shops long before they became popular. "We would haul home the most fabulous dress-up booty—gorgeous tulle and chiffon evening gowns and fur stoles, high-heeled shoes, gloves, and fabulous costume jewelry to complete the look. As the years passed, my enchantment blossomed into a full-blown fashion addiction, which still shows little sign of abatement. My inability to leave a terrific vintage designer piece on the rack has been held in check only by my lack of storage space.

"Thanks to the Internet, I can now offer my treasures to other appreciative souls who value the nostalgic charms of wearing vintage apparel and accessories and making them uniquely theirs," said Redden. Designers you will find are Yves Saint Laurent, Anne Fogarty, Mollie Parnis, Giorgio di Sant'Angelo, Anne Klein, Leonard, Donald Brooks, Elsa Peretti, Christian Dior, Pierre Cardin, and many others.

Her favorite era? "The '30s, because the style was so feminine and romantic, but I like the '70s as well, because I can relive my fashion deprived youth by dressing in all the cool clothes my mom wouldn't let me buy back then."

Current offerings include: a '60s Bill Blass princess ball gown in silk lamé with an empire bodice and huge painted flowers; a '60s Courrèges kelly green sleeveless shift dress with strategically placed white zippers (quintessential Courrèges!); and a '50s Gucci brown handbag with tiger-eye clasp.

SAZZ VINTAGE CLOTHING
$–$$

www.sazzvintage.com

Owner: Amanda
Return Policy: Refund within ten days

Sazz Vintage Clothing's specialty are Western clothes and '50s rockabilly styles. "The rockabilly scene is a rich music family all over the world that draws from a mix of rock 'n' roll, country, blues, and honky-tonk," says

Amanda. "It's all about dancing, drinking, loving, and fighting. Elvis is still king. Men wear their white T-shirts tight and their Western or '50s shirts with the sleeves rolled high. Women swing in darling '50s frou-frou crinoline party dresses or pout-so-pretty in pencil skirts; tight little sweaters; and saddle shoes. Life is in fast gear. Kats are expected to have grease under their nails, and kittens make tattoos sexy in a completely new way."

Sazz carries H Bar C and Rockmount RanchWear (fancy Western), Jonathan Logan (1950s–60s dresses), Levi's, Wrangler, Miller, Authentic Western Youngbloods, and Karman. Current offerings include: a royal blue H Bar C gabardine Western shirt from the '50s with multi-colored embroidery along both front and back yokes and the collar; a '50s white and pink, flowered taffeta party dress with an attached inner crinoline, spaghetti straps, and Talon zipper; and a dead stock '50s men's bright maroon, acetate, long-sleeve lounge shirt.

THE SNOB, INC.

$–$$$

www.thesnob.net *or* www.thesnob.co.uk

> *Owner:* Rula Carr
> *Return Policy:* All sales final

The Snob, Inc. offers Chanel, Gucci, Prada, Hermès, Louis Vuitton, Ferragamo, St. John, Ungaro, Donna Karan, Dolce & Gabbana, Michael Kors, Dana Buchman, Calvin Klein, DKNY, Kaspar, Ellen Tracy, and more, because "high-end, designer name clothing is in demand. Customer focus has been and continues to be our key to success," said Carr. "Our customers are individuals with specific fashion tastes and desires. At The Snob we carefully cultivate customer relationships over time and maintain individual 'wish lists' that allow us to fulfill many of our customers' desires."

For Carr, a British native, The Snob, Inc. is not just a business success but also the fulfillment of a childhood dream. "I was born and raised in London where my mother was a seamstress, and I grew to appreciate fine clothes." Carr has turned what started out as a hobby stemming from a childhood fascination with beautiful clothes into a business with national contacts attracting supplies of designer clothing from around the country and beyond. Not that Carr is immune to the charm of vintage. Her favorite collectable? A Hermès vintage alligator handbag dating from the early '70s.

THE STOCK EXCHANGE
$–$$

www.viewthebest.com/stockexchange

> *Owner:* Meg Thomas
> *Return Policy:* All sales final

The Stock Exchange was established in 1985 and, despite the many inquiries, "does not deal in consignment of livestock," says Thomas. "Our on-line store," says Thomas, "is being used as a personal shopper service for lovers of designer and collectible clothing, contemporary and vintage. We do offer listings of items from time to time but have been most successful with answering requests for specific designers, sizes, or other items. We have handled women's consigned items from individuals, used and new (over 8,900 accounts). Most large estates are on consignment, and we have consignment arriving from people from across the U.S. every day."

Name brands carried run the gamut: Gap, Old Navy, Trina Turk, Gucci, Prada, Pucci, Kate Spade, Rena Lange, Escada, Flax, Blue Fish, Abercrombie & Fitch, Manolo Blahnik, J.Crew, Armani, Chanel, Diesel, Earl Jeans, and other high-end designers. Some of the items currently in stock include: a cigar case purse (made from a real cigar case) with gold fixtures for the handle and closure; a Blue Fish hand-painted, green cotton piece with flowerpots, gardening tools, and seed packets; and Emanuel Ungaro boots edged in feathers around the ankles. Thomas' favorite find? A Pucci robe in celery, periwinkle, and soft gray in immaculate condition. "We also have Gucci purses in the original boxes from the '70s. The consignor was a nice lady who used to work in New York and would shop on her lunch break. She saved everything...and if she every used any of these things it would amaze me."

Thomas' favorite period goes along with what's hot at any given time. "I like '70s print tops and Pucci items a lot. I also like '40s suits and once found a great Norman Norell navy evening gown from the late '50s. It was made from Duchess satin and had a square neck." Her favorite consignor has over 500 pairs of Manolo Blahnik shoes. "A shopaholic, she consigns hundreds of items at a time and we have to take rolling racks out to her car just to get everything in."

TANGERINE BOUTIQUE
$

www.tangerineboutique.com

> **Owner:** Melody King
> **Return Policy:** Refund within three days less shipping and $5 restocking fee

Tangerine Boutique owner Melody King spent years as a dress and hat maker, thus her interest in flattering, unique, and nicely constructed clothing. "I am a textile snob, so I look for beautiful or unique fabric in the garments." Designers carried include Mollie Parnis, Adele Simpson, Carrie Couture, Yves Saint Laurent, Bonnie Cashin, Kenzo, Anne Fogarty, and more.

The most interesting pieces she's collected? An antique hand-embroidered robe from Morocco of fine red wool with the "most exquisite flowers. I wear it over cigarette pants with a camisole," says King. She loves the '30s purely for design reasons—the use of bias cuts and gorgeous handwork. "I like the '40s for myself because the clothing is flattering to a curvy shape."

Current offerings include: a 1918 black and metallic gold evening cape; a '60s gray boucle dress and jacket ensemble trimmed with chinchilla; and a very funky mod two-piece outfit complete with halter-top vest in hot pink and purple.

A Victorian Elegance

$$–$$$

www.victorianelegance.com

> **Owner:** Bill and Donna Barr
> **Return Policy:** Refunds within two days less shipping

A Victorian Elegance offers early Victorian–1970s treasures, although the Barr's most admire the 1850s–1880s for the "wonderful workmanship and style." The most interesting pieces they've collected are a French label Edwardian beaded gown in its original box and a black gown that belonged to Cher. Check out their wedding site (www.vintagewedding.com) for everything a bride and groom could possibly need.

Current offerings include: a white cotton and ribbon camisole, "pretty enough to wear as a summer blouse," with a wide neckline gathered with blue ribbon; a '30s brown dress/slip jacket with the original rust-colored underslip, net dress, and net jacket; and a '30s bias cut black taffeta gown with large pink roses.

Vintage Baubles

$–$$

www.VintageBaubles.com

> **Owner:** P.L.W. (Pamela) Browne
> **Return Policy:** Refund within 24 hours less shipping and 15% restocking

Vintage Baubles carries contemporary resale such as A.B.S., Ballinger Gold, Bill Blass, Bruno Magli, Calvin Klein, Carmen Marc Valvo, Carole Little, Christian Dior, DKNY, Fabrikant, Louis Feraud, Ferragamo, Genny, Givenchy, Jaeger, Jones New York, Michael Kors, Linda Allard/Ellen Tracy, Marie St. Claire, Oscar de la Renta, Rodier, Sadimara, Saks, Scaasi, Tahari, Ungaro, Victor Costa, Diane von Furstenberg, Adrienne Vittadini, and Stewart Weitzman.

Vintage labels include Adolph Shaman, Andre Jovan, Badgley Mischka, Bill Blass, Burberry, Calvin Klein, Carolina Herrera, Castleberry, Christian Dior, Escada, Etienne Aigner, Fendi, Louis Feraud, Ferragamo, Fiandaca, Gucci, Jantzen, Halston, KJL, Lillie Rubin, Lilly Daché, Pierre Cardin, Pucci, Sasson, Oscar de la Renta, Scaasi, St. John, Todd Oldham, Victor Costa, Vanity Fair, Victoria Royal Ltd., Whiting & Davis, and Yves Saint Laurent.

Browne specializes in high-quality vintage designer clothing and accessories and offers only those items that are in excellent condition and exhibit exceptional fabrication, workmanship, and tailoring. She acquires items from "estate sales, antique shops, auctions, private collections, thrift shops, garage sales, and flea markets in the hope that women will incorporate these unique and chic designer vintage items in their personal wardrobes, create their own individual style, and preserve the items for future generations to enjoy."

Browne loves to collect and wear hats. "So I was thrilled when my mother gave me my great-grandmother Korner's 1880s Gainsborough hat to add to my personal collection about 20 years ago. The tan straw hat is handmade with a gorgeous brown velvet band and a large, vertical velvet and lace plume." If Browne had to select only one favorite period, it would be the '60s, "because I love simple, elegant clothing with clean, lean lines that can be accessorized easily with great jewelry, handbags, and hats. But I also love beaded dresses and lingerie from the '20s and '30s—as well as jackets, coats, beaded sweaters, and accessories from the '40s and '50s."

Current offerings include: a '70s Adele Simpson timeless black and white fully lined knit suit; a '60s double-breasted Krasner's Buffalo "carpet" coat with black faux fur trimmed collar, cuffs, and hem; and a '70s Pendleton riding jacket.

"Never underestimate the dramatic impact of a pair of gorgeous vintage gloves. Women use their hands expressively more than they know, and so relatively inexpensively they can add a flash of Schiaparelli pink or lemon yellow to that little black dress."

—ROBERT TURTURICE, COSTUME DESIGNER FOR BATMAN AND ROBIN

VINTAGE COUTURE
$–$$$

www.vintagecouture.com

Owner: Lynda Latner
Return Policy: Refund within ten days less shipping and 20% restocking

Vintage Couture specializes in vintage designer clothing from U.S. and European design houses like Cardin, Heim, Yves Saint Laurent, Stephen Burrows, Lanz, Halston, Bottega Veneta, Missoni, Molyneux, Courréges, Fabiani, Galliano, Madame Grés, and Galanos. "Each piece consigned to me by a client is like a child waiting for the right family to adopt it," says Latner. "Each piece has sentimental value to the owner. They saved and cherished it for so many years that it requires sensitivity and consideration to move on to its next home. The right fit is about more than just size!"

A client in Montreál, who had saved all her significant purchases from 1947 to 1961, gave Latner 37 pieces of couture clothing. "Part of the collection was so spectacular that I worked with the client to donate two exceptional dresses to the Royal Ontario Museum in Toronto for their couture collection. In my opinion, the best item was a 1951 black lace Balenciaga couture balloon gown that had been featured in *Harpers Bazaar*, September 1951 issue.

"My personal favorite is the '70s. I lived in England from 1970 until '76, the height of the London Look with Mary Quant, Bill Gibb, Ossie Clark, and Biba. They brought fashion to the people at prices that everyone could afford. It was colorful, hip, bohemian, punk, mod—it was all about freedom of expression with great style and modern fabrics," says Latner.

Current stock includes: a late '50s Balenciaga mustard linen peplum style suit, a plaid wool suit, and a black cloque silk draped black two piece evening dress; a Dior Summer 1959 black and white checkered suit and Winter 1961 brown wool cropped jacket with leopard silk lining and leopard silk caplet style top; a Youthquake London mid-'60s bright green minidress with stoplight motif on the front; and an Irene Galitzine op art heavy silk suit from the early '60s with a pumpkin orange cowl neck top.

There are several unusual Italian and French crocodile bags, clutches, totes, and day bags in excellent condition. As part of the normal inventory, you can always find Pucci silk knits, Gucci logo leather goods, Chanel shoes in perfect condition, as well as vintage dead stock exotic shoes by Andrea Pfister and Maud Frizon. Chanel suits from the famous Scooby Doo 1994 collection and early '50s couture Chanel dresses and accessories are always appearing for sale on the web site.

VINTAGE VIXEN CLOTHING COMPANY

$–$$$

www.vintagevixen.com

> **Owner:** April Girtman
> **Return Policy:** Refund within three days less shipping and 15% restocking

Vintage Vixen Clothing Company specializes in variety rather than a particular era or look. Girtman knows that customers visit for different reasons, so she provides a variety of lines, from designer clothing to funky costume-oriented pieces to simply great looking wardrobe items. Girtman carries Geoffrey Beene, Oleg Cassini, Lilly Pulitzer, Christian Dior, Pierre Cardin, Ferragamo, Oscar de la Renta, Pucci, early Anne Klein, Mollie Parnis, Donald Brooks, Alfred Shaheen, Enid Collins, and the Vested Gentress.

The most interesting garment Girtman has ever collected? "I don't personally keep clothing as a rule, because I want to offer the best to my customers, not stow special items away. I do find certain details special, like '20s ribbon embroidery or other impossible-to-duplicate trims and fabrics. I also particularly enjoy unusual cuts and seaming in a garment. Right now I could single out an early '40s men's suit jacket, a common style for the time, except that there's a yellowed bit of red, white, and blue ribbon pinned to the lapel. This was such a poignant reminder of times past for me, that a world war happened only a couple of generations ago."

The '30s is Girtman's favorite era. "There was a great deal of social upheaval in this decade, and I believe fashion acted and reacted accordingly. The result was breathtaking and svelte in the deluxe salons of the day, though the average person's wardrobe included feedsack and cheer-me-up Depression era prints. Such a contrast! The really interesting detail is that women of the era, whether rich or poor, both used strange and quirky motifs in their clothing, such as Schiaparelli's bizarre 1930s showings."

Current offerings include: a '70s Diane von Furstenberg tulip print dress with original tags labeled "Diane von Furstenberg MADE IN ITALY"; a "fantastic" pink and lime cotton sun shift with Jamaican scenes; and a late '50s Calypso daisy print blouse.

THE WAY WE WORE
$–$$

thewaywewore.net

> **Owner:** Pam Nunnally
> **Return Policy:** Exchange only

The Way We Wore specializes in "anything that is old and unique," says Nunnally. "I also specialize in the certain things that happen to be trendy at any given time. Right now the '60s and '70s are the most popular. The younger generation buys this merchandise for their everyday fashion and my older clientele gets it for costuming, theme parties, and Halloween." Although her stock is always changing, Nunnally consistently carries Pucci, Christian Dior, and Pauline Trigère gathered from "estates, shopping, and digging everywhere I go!"

Nunnally's most interesting piece ever collected was a "great '40s or maybe '50s Western suit. It was chartreuse green with embroidery and rhinestones and absolutely gorgeous! I should have never sold that!" Her favorite? "I love the '40s! Everything from that period is so classy, and the fabrics are wonderful and very wearable."

Current offerings include: a '60s Emilio Pucci cotton sundress from his signature psychedelic print line; a flowing, golden yellow, '30s silk chiffon and beaded ball gown; and a 1960–70s black fringe jumpsuit—perfect for a Cher outfit.

SHOPPING THE
eXPOS

CALENDAR OF SHOWS:

Barrows Show Promotional, Ltd.: P.O. Box 141, Portland, CT 06480; (203) 342-2540. January, June, and November shows in West Hartford, CT.

Brimfield Associates: P.O. Box 1800, Ocean City, NY 08226; (609) 926-1800. March and October shows at the Atlantic City Convention Hall, Atlantic City, NJ.

Caskey Lees: P.O. Box 1409, Topanga, CA 90290; (310) 455-2886. One clothing and textile show each year, date and location vary.

Cat's Pajamas: 125 W. Main St., Dundee, IL 60118; (708) 428-8368. March and October shows at Hemmens Auditorium, 150 Dexter Crt., Elgin, IL 60120.

Deco to '50s: 1217 Waterview Dr., Mill Valley, CA 94941; (415) 383-3008. Two deco shows each year in San Francisco.

Great Eastern Productions: R.D. #2, Box 141, Zionsville, PA 18092; (215) 967-2181. March show in the Agricultural Hall at the Allentown Fairgrounds: 302 N. 17th St. Allentown, PA 18104.

JR Promotions: (509) 375-5273. Runs vintage shows in Seattle.

Love, Ellen: (914) 988-9609. Runs shows and sells materials.

David M. & Peter J. Mancuso, Inc.: Professional Show Management: P.O. Box 667, New Hope, PA 18938. February show at the Patrick Henry Inn: 249 E. York St., Williamsburg, VA 23187; (757) 229-9540.

The Maven Company, Inc. & The Young Management Company: P.O. Box 1538, Waterbury, CT 06721; (213) 758-3880; www.mavencompany.com. Holds multiple vintage clothing and jewelry shows each year in the Northeast U.S.

Metropolitan Art & Antiques Pavilion: 110 W. 19th St., New York, NY 10011; (212) 463-0200. Fall, winter, and spring shows in the Pavilion.

Molly's Vintage Promotions: 194 Amity St., Amherst, MA 01002; (413) 549-6446. September show at the Holiday Inn: 245 Whiting Farms Rd., Holyoke,

MA 01040; (413) 533-8443. April vintage and textile show at 200 Fifth Club: 200 Fifth Ave., New York, NY 10010; (212) 675-2080.

Nadia: P.O. Box 156, Flourtown, PA 19301; (215) 643-1396. November and February shows in the ballroom at the Adams Mark Grand Hotel: 4000 City Ave., Philadelphia, PA 19131; (215) 581-5000.

Oldies but Goodies: Hankins, NY; (914) 877-5272. Vanity items, shows only.

Renningers Promotions: 27 Bensinger Dr., Schuylkill Haven, PA 17971; (717) 385-0104. February and March shows at the Valley Forge Convention Center: 1160 First Ave., King of Prussia, PA 19406; (610) 337-2000.

Show Associates: P.O. Box 729, Cape Neddick, ME 03902; (207) 439-2334. Holds vintage clothing and textile shows in Sturbridge, MA.

Somewhere In Time Promotions: P.O. Box 88892, Seattle, WA 98138; (206) 531-4194. September and March shows at the Seattle Center Flag Pavilion: First Ave. and Republican at Seattle Center, Seattle, WA 98109; (206) 684-7200.

Stella Show Management Co.: 163 Terrace St., Haworth, NJ 07641; (201) 384-0010; www.stellashows.com. Holds multiple antique shows each year with many vintage dealers from the East Coast.

The Williamsburg Vintage Fashion & Accessories Show: Williamsburg, VA; (215) 862-5828. Held the last week of February.

Vintage Expositions: Box 391, Alamo, CA 94507; (415) 822-7227. January and September show at the Oakland Convention Center: Broadway and Tenth St., Oakland, CA 94607. February, October, and December shows at the Santa Monica Civic Auditorium: 1855 Main St., Santa Monica, CA 90401. March show at Concourse Exhibition Center: 635 Eighth St., San Francisco, CA 94103.

VINTAGE AUCTIONS:

Butterfields: 220 San Bruno Ave., San Francisco, CA 94103; (415) 861-7500. Fine jewelry and watches only.

Christie's: 20 Rockefeller Plaza, New York, NY 10020; (212) 636-2000; or 360 N. Camden Dr., Beverly Hills, CA 90210; (310) 385-2600.

Christie's East: 219 E. 67th St., New York, NY 10021; (212) 606-0400.

Ritchie's Auctioneers & Appraisers: 288 King St., Toronto, ON MSA 1K4; (416) 364-1864 or (800) 364-3210.

Wescheler's: 909 E St. Northwest, Washington, D.C. 20004; (202) 628-1281.

William Doyle Galleries: 175 E. 87th St., New York, NY 10128; (212) 427-2730.

Sotheby's: 1334 York Ave., New York, NY 10021; (212) 606-7000. According to the *Los Angeles Times*, a beaded Dolce & Gabbana bra worn by Madonna during her Girlie Tour sold for a record of $23,850 during Sotheby's two-week on-line auction.

Ebay: www.ebay.com. Celebrities often team up with Ebay to auction personal items with proceeds going to their favorite charities. Winona Ryder, for example, auctioned pieces she had worn to special events and collectibles that had belonged to stars such as Joan Crawford and Audrey Hepburn.

APPENDIX

MUSEUMS

The Art Institute of Chicago: Michigan Ave. at Adama St., Chicago, IL 60603; (312) 443-3600.

Arizona Costume Institute: The Phoenix Art Museum, 1625 N. Central Ave., Phoenix, AZ 85004; (602) 257-1222; www.phxart.org.

Brooklyn Museum: Eastern Parkway, Brooklyn, NY 11238; (718) 638-5000.

Chicago Historical Society: Clark St. at North Ave., Chicago, IL 60614; (312) 642-4600.

Cincinnati Art Museum: Eden Park, Cincinnati, OH 45202; (513) 721-5204.

Cooper-Hewitt Museum: Smithsonian Museum of Design, 2 E. 91st St., New York, NY 10128; (212) 860-6868.

The Fashion Institute of Technology: The Edward C. Blum Design Laboratory, 227 W. 27th St., New York, NY 10001; (212) 217-7000.

Indianapolis Museum of Art: 1200 W. 38th St., Indianapolis, IN 46208; (317) 923-1331; www.ima/art.org.

Los Angeles County Museum of Art: Costume and Textile Department, 5905 Wilshire Blvd., Los Angeles, CA 90036; (213) 857-6000; www.lacma.org.

Metropolitan Museum of Art Costume Institute: Fifth Ave. at 82nd St., New York, NY 10028; (212) 879-5500 ext. 3908; www.metmuseum.org.

M. H. de Young Memorial Museum: Golden Gate Park, San Francisco, CA 94118; (415) 558-2887.

The Museum of Fine Arts: 465 Huntington Ave., Boston, MA 02115; (617) 267-9300; www.mfa.org.

Museum of the City of New York: 1220 Fifth Ave., New York, NY 10029; (212) 534-1672; www.mcny.org.

The National Museum of American History—Costume Division: Smithsonian Institute, Washington D.C. 20560; (202) 357-3185.

The Oakland Museum: 1000 Oak St., Oakland, CA 94607; (415) 273-3842.

Philadelphia Museum of Art: Benjamin Franklin Parkway, Box 7646, Philadelphia, PA 19101; (215) 763-8100.

The Texas Fashion Collection: North Texas State University, Denton, TX 76203; (817) 565-2732.

University of Washington Historical Costume & Textile Collection: Seattle, WA 98195; (206) 543-1739.

Wadsworth Atheneum: 600 Main St., Hartford, CT 06103; (203) 278-2670.

Western Reserve Historical Society Chisholm Hall Costume Wing: 10825 East Blvd., Cleveland, OH 44106; (216) 721-5722.

ORGANIZATIONS

The Costume and Textile Group of New Jersey: P.O. Box 8623, Woodcliff Lake, NY 07675.

The Costume Society of America: P.O. Box 73, 55 Edgewater Dr., Earleville, MD 21919; (800) CSA-9447; www.costumesocietyamerica.com.

International Old Lacers, Inc.: 2409 S. Ninth St., Lafayette, IN 47905.

National Association of Resale & Thrift Shops (NART'S): P.O. Box 80707, St. Clair Shores, MI 48080; (800) 544-0751; www.narts.org. With over 1,000 members, this association serves thrift, resale, and consignment shops of all types by providing educational and professional development for store owners/managers, promoting communication within the industry, and building public recognition of the business. NART'S offers an on-line merchandise search and consumer information links.

PUBLICATIONS

Newsletters:

Bustle: P.O. Box 361, Midtown Station, New York, NY 10019; (212) 228-6137. The quarterly of the Ladies' Tea & Rhetoric Society.

The Costume and Textile Group of New Jersey Newsletter: P.O. Box 8623, Woodcliff Lake, NJ 07675.

The Echoes Report: Deco Echoes Publications, P.O. Box 2321, Mashpee, MA 02649.

The Lady's Gallery: P.O. Box 1761, Independence, MO 64055.

The Perspicacious Woman On-Line: 67 E. Oak St. 6th Floor, Chicago, IL 60611; (312) 943-8880; www.daisyshop.com. Published by The Daisy Shop (see p. xxx)

Vintage!: P.O. Box 412, Alamo, CA 94507; (707) 793-0773. The publication of the Federation of Vintage Fashion.

Vintage Clothing Newsletter: P.O. Box 1422, Corvalis, OR 97339.

The Vintage Connection: 904 N. 65 St., Springfield, OR 97478-7021.

The Vintage Gazette: 194 Amity St., Amherst, MA 01002; (413) 549-6446.

Magazines

Ornament: P.O. Box 2349, San Marcos, CA 92079-2349; (800) 888-8950.

Piecework: Interweave Press Inc., 201 E. Fourth St., Loveland, CO 80537; (303) 669-7672.

Victoria: P.O. Box 7150, Red Oak, IA 51597; (800) 876-8696.

A-line: A shape of skirts and dresses that is fitted at the top and flares out at the hem in the form of the letter "A."

Bakelite: Trade name for a synthetic material used in buttons, buckles, bracelets, and other adornments.

Bat wing sleeves: See dolman sleeves.

Beret: A soft cap with a round flat crown of varying widths, often made of felt or wool.

Bermuda: As in Bermuda shorts, short trousers first worn in Bermuda.

Bias cut: Cutting fabric across the grain at a 45-degree angle to produce a closely draped garment.

Blouson: A "bloused" garment; fullness caught into a smaller fitted piece of fabric, such as a full cut top gathered into a fitted skirt at the waist or hips.

Boucle: French for "buckled," boucle yarn is tightly curled, when used in fabric the surface has a looped appearance.

Brocade: Fabric with a raised, often floral, design.

Caftan: Full-length unfitted flowing garment with sleeves, based on garments worn in eastern Mediterranean countries.

Capri pants: Women's pants, often made of cotton, straight-legged and close-fitting, ending just below the knee.

Cartridge pleats: Developed in 15th century Europe to enable large sleeves and skirts to be gathered into the bodice; the pleats are round folds of fabric, resembling the bullet sleeves in a cartridge belt.

Chemise: Women's undergarment that hangs straight down from the shoulder straps; basically an unfitted "slip."

Clam digger: Women's casual pants, worn fairly tight and ending just above the ankle.

Cloche: A close-fitting woman's hat with a high, round crown and narrow brim worn low over the eyes, popularized by flappers in the 1920s.

Cotton piqué: A cotton fabric in either a corded, waffle, or diamond weave; most often used for stiff collars and cuffs.

Cowl collar: A cowl was originally a monk's hood; fashion adapted it into a loose collar or drape of material in front and/or behind the neck.

Crêpe de Chine: A soft, lightweight fabric, usually silk, sometimes slightly crinkled in appearance.

Dashikis: A T-shaped cotton garment of African origin, worn over pants.

Dead stock: Merchandise that was never used, usually vintage, and has once again been put up for sale.

Djellabas: A loose long-sleeved hooded garment worn in northern Africa.

Dolman sleeve: A sleeve that is wide at the shoulder and narrows to the wrist; sometimes an extension of the bodice with no seaming.

Empire waist: A waistline placed anywhere from slightly above the natural waistline to just below the bust.

Faggoted seams: Two hemmed edges joined with an openwork stitch.

Fishtail: A train on a gown or costume that flares into the shape of a fishtail.

Gabardine: A tightly woven fabric with a diagonal ribbed effect, often used for suits, coats, and uniforms.

Gauntlet: Originally gloves that medieval knights wore to protect their hands; now gloves that extend over the wrist and forearm.

Guayaberas: Men's boxy sport shirts, usually made of cotton and worn untucked over the trouser; originated in Cuba.

Headdress: Anything that adorns the head, such as ribbons, flowers, combs, bonnets, etc.

Jerkin: Dating from the 16th century and used only in reference to period clothing, a fitted sleeveless jacket or short coat.

Kimono: A Japanese garment; loose robe with very wide sleeves fastened with a wide sash.

Lettuce finishing: Thread stitched on the raw edge of fabric, causes a wavy hem.

Little black dress: A term used to denote the perfect black afternoon or cocktail dress; stylish, simple, classic, and a necessity in any well-dressed woman's closet.

Mackinaw: A hip-length coat, often with plaid lining, made of heavy wool.

Maillot: From the French meaning "tights," a women's tight one-piece bathing suit.

Middy blouse: Women's blouse copied from the sailor's white top with a navy collar.

Mohair: Fabric made from the long silky hair of the Angora goat.

Moiré: A fabric that reflects light in an irregular wavy pattern, similar to the appearance of gasoline on water.

Overblouse: A blouse designed to hang untucked over pants or skirts.

Pavé: Sparkling stones set close together for decoration on purses and accessories.

Pedal pushers: Women's trousers that are fitted, tapered, and hemmed just below the knee.

Peplum: A flounce or ruffle that hangs from a women's blouse or jacket over the hips.

Pierrot ruffs: A ruffled collar like that worn by the French pantomime character Pierrot.

Pillbox: A small round hat that resembles a pillbox, made popular by Jackie Kennedy.

Platform sole: An elevating sole that runs evenly along the full length of the shoe, anywhere from one inch on up—the sky's the limit.

Ply: A strand of yarn. Four ply, for example, indicates the thickness of the weave as four strands.

Pochette: From the French meaning "little pocket," it refers to a small handbag.

Poncho: An unseamed piece of fabric, often square, with a hole in the center for the head. First worn in Mexico, now it often refers to a plastic raincovering.

Princess line: Seams running the length of a garment creating a form-fitting shape throughout the upper torso. In dresses it may continue to the hem, fitting like an hourglass or flaring out into an A-line.

Ready-to-wear: A garment not made to order; made in quantity for the mass consumer in a range of sizes.

Ruche: A strip of fabric, usually fluted, pleated, or gathered and used for trim.

Shirring: Fabric drawn together along two seams creating an ornamental gathering.

Shirting: A fabric used to make shirts, usually a fine cotton or linen.

Shirtwaist: A tailored blouse or dress for women in the style of men's shirts.

Sling-back: A woman's shoe with an open back and a strap around the heel.

Snood: A popular 1940s item, a small hairnet-like accessory, often crocheted, and worn over a bun at the nape of the neck.

Taffeta: A smooth, shiny fabric, most often used for formalwear. The best quality is made of silk, but it can be made of polyester.

Tam: Short for "tam o'shanter," a hat of Scottish origins with a tight headband and a wide, loose crown that drapes around the head and sports a tuft a wool at its center.

Ticking: Strong fabric made of linen or cotton, often used in upholstery.

Toque: A soft triangular cap, fitted to the head and coming to a blunt point at the crown.

Trapeze: Shirt that is fitted at the upper torso and either hangs straight or flares outward in to an "A" shape at the waist.

Trapunto: A decorative quilted effect where a design is created by stitching two pieces of fabric together and stuffing it with cotton batting.

Trompe l'oeil: French for "decieve the eye;" something used to create an illusion.

Turban: Originally referred to the long scarf worn wrapped around the head in many Moslem cultures; now any headwear made from fabric twisted around the head.

Ultrasuede: Trade name for knitted fabric finished to resemble suede.

Wedge sandal: A sandal or shoe with a solid sole that is thicker at the heel than the toe.

Yoke: The portion of the garment that is fitted to the shoulders or hips and from which the rest of the garment hangs.

Zoot suit: Born around 1935 in Harlem nightclubs and made famous by teens in the early '40s, a men's suit of exaggerated proportions. Pants are baggy on top and tight at the ankle and jackets are wide-shouldered and almost knee-length.

SELECTED BIBLIOGRAPHY

Callan, Georgina O'Hara. *The Thames and Hudson Dictionary of Fashion and Fashion Designers.* New York: Thames and Hudson, 1998.

Carnegy, Vicky. *Fashion of a Decade: The 1980s.* New York: Facts On File, Inc., 1990.

Dubin, Tiffany. "The Power of Personal Style." *Ladies Home Journal* Nov. 2001: 120.

Dubin, Tiffany and Ann E. Berman. *Vintage Style: Buying and Wearing Classic Vintage Clothes.* New York: Harper Collins, 2000.

"Eye Scoop." *W* 3 April 1989: 6

Ganem, Mark. "A Feminine Oomph." *W* 20 Feb. 1989: 68.

---. "Milano the New France." *W* 3 April 1989: 50.

Herald, Jacqueline. *Fashion of a Decade: The 1920s.* New York: Facts On File, Inc., 1991.

Houck, Catherine. *The Fashion Encyclopedia: An Essential Guide to Everything You Need to Know About Clothes.* New York: St. Martin's Press, 1982.

Howell, Georgina. *In Vogue: Sixty Years of Celebrities and Fashion from British Vogue.* London: Penguin, 1975.

Lindstrom, Jan. "Designing Hollywood: Reverence of Things Past." *Daily Variety* 26 April 2000: 1–9.

Lintermans, Gloria. *Cheap Chic: A Guide to LA's Resale Boutiques.* Los Angeles: A.Lintermans Publishers, 1990.

Markwell, Lisa. "Crown Prince of Fashion." *ELLE British Edition* Dec. 1988: 70.

Martin, Richard and Harold Kida. *Jocks and Nerds: Men's Style in the Twentieth Century.* New York: Rizzoli, 1990.

Mason, Elizabeth. *Valuable Vintage.* New York: Henry Holt & Company, 2001.

McDowell, Colin. *McDowells' Directory of Twentieth Century Fashion.* New Jersey: Prentice-Hall, Inc., 1985.

Mower, Sarah. "Emperor Armani." *Vogue British Edition* Dec. 1988: 342.

Mueller, Cookie. "It's Been Twenty-Five Years." Details Dec. 1988: 163.

O'Donnol, Shirley Miles. *American Costume: A Source Book for the Stage Costumer, 1915-1970.* Bloomington: Indiana University Press, 1982.

Peacock, John. *Fashion Accessories: The Complete 20th Century Sourcebook.* London: Thames & Hudson, 2000.

Picken, Mary Brooks. *A Dictionary of Costume and Fashion: Historic and Modern.* Mineola: Dover Publications, Inc., 1986.

Smith, Pamela. *Vintage Fashion & Fabrics.* New York: Alliance Publishing, Inc., 1995.

Thim, Dennis. "The Word From Paris, Bohan/Dior." *W* 6 March 1989: 112.

---. "The Word From Paris, Montana." *W* 6 March 1989: 120.

Tolkein, Tracy. *Dressing Up Vintage.* New York: Rizzoli International Publishers, Inc., 2000.

Watkins, Josephine Ellis. *Who's Who in Fashion.* New York: Fairchild Publications, Inc., 1975.

Watson, Linda. *20th Century Fashion: 100 Years of Style by Decade & Designer.* Broomall: Chelsea House, 2000.

Weil, Christa. *Secondhand Chic: Finding Fabulous Fashion at Consignment, Vintage, and Thrift Stores.* New York: Pocket Books, 1999.

ALPHABETICAL INDEX

INDEX BY PRICE

DIANA EDEN is an award-winning film and television costume designer. Her work includes *Family Law*, *A League of Their Own* (Emmy nomination), and *Ned and Stacey*. She's dressed George Clooney, Anjelica Huston, Ann-Margret, Tony Danza, Melissa Gilbert, Jamie Kennedy, and Alyson Hannigan. She lives (and shops) in Los Angeles and Toronto, Canada.

GLORIA LINTERMANS is the former internationally syndicated fashion and beauty columnist of *Looking Great*, also the title of her former radio and cable TV shows. She lives (and shops) in Los Angeles.